A Dog's Tale

A Dog's Tale

by Pepper

with Ron Wormser

March 2017
Carmel, California

The stories told in these pages are based on the author's personal experience, perceptions, and memory. Suggested corrections might be sent to the author through PepperSpeaks.com.

A Dog's Tale

All Rights Reserved

© 2017 by Ron Wormser

ISBN-13: 978-1542895972
ISBN-10: 1542895979

Printed in the United States of America

Table of Contents

A Dog's Tale

Acknowledgments

A Dog's Tale would not have been possible had it not been for Bonnie Read Wormser who suggested it was time we get a dog, for Dick Dye who unintentionally created circumstances that gave birth to the idea, for Naomi Graffman who provided encouragement at an early stage, for numerous friends who read print shop copies and offered more encouragement, for Gene Fedors who insisted and persisted in the notion that the book be published, for Marci Bracco Cain who lent her considerable efforts and talent to the venture, for Tony Seton who believed enough to commit to its publication and kind enough to lend invaluable editorial guidance, and most especially for my dear wife Marian's patience, encouragement, support, editorial assistance and above all being my true best friend. I am indebted and grateful to them all.

This book is dedicated to Pepper who gave me so much for so long.

<u>*Publisher's Note*</u>

I met with Ron Wormser to talk about the Fourth Estate and funding a training program to produce top quality journalists. We got together again. And in no time, our conversation rose to a higher level...our canine friends. No, we didn't take out our wallets to exchange photos of our loved ones, but it was close. I did share with him that my favorite bumper sticker read "Wife and dog missing. Reward for dog."

Indeed, I had once married a woman largely because I'd met her dog. His was a big yellow Lab mix named Buster. We were instantly fast friends. Five and half years later, when the wife and I were ready to call it quits, I left for three weeks to find a new home. When I returned to get my things, I said good-bye to my dear friend.

Buster was around 15 at that time, and ailing. Four days after I left, he was gone. He had waited for me to come back to say good-bye. Thirteen years later, I remember him with more love than I have for the two-leggers who have exited from my life.

So when Ron asked me for suggestions about publishing options for *A Dog's Tale* – the book he had written with his best friend, Pepper – of course I needed to read it. Having read it, I wanted to be its publisher. I did so without trepidation because Ron knows how to write, but I was more than delighted with how well he could put thoughts and feelings – his own and Pepper's – into words.

This book is for everyone who has had a relationship with a dog, and all those who have missed out but need to understand.

Tony Seton

Author's Note

This is the story of my life seen from about six inches off the ground. From my perspective, almost everything's looking up.

While it's true that not every dog gets the chance to chronicle his life's story, I thought it high time to put paper to use more creatively than the usual option you rather insistently offer.

Of course the pet section of your bookstore is overflowing with tomes and your folklore brims with allegedly 'real' but actually imagined facts about us. There are even television shows, and on the educational channel to boot, that either show us in storybook settings or which try to train you how to train us.

But all this is based solely on your speculation as if you actually know what goes on between our adorable – irresistible – must be scratched - ears. So it's about time that one of us speaks out. After all you've been trying to get us to speak for a long time.

Spoiler alert: You may not always like what you are about to learn. You may find yourself more comfortable with your folklore and imaginings. If so, read no further. Do not pass GO. And do not seek a refund.

If on the other hand, you want to learn about a dog's life directly from the source, read on. My hope is that my literary scratching will illuminate and enrich one of life's true wonders: the special, precious bond between our two species.

I hope you will find the journey as amusing as it is informative. I also hope you will put this down at the end with a greater appreciation and respect for your best friends.

Pepper
New York City, 1988

Assistant's Note

A Dog's Tale was begun in the early fall of 1988 with a particular objective: to share the view of my pet companion, a miniature Schnauzer named Pepper, of what it was like to grow up and live in mid-town Manhattan. And what better locale for such a story than The Big Apple, a place where reality is often stranger than fiction?

It was important that it be his book, told in his voice from his perspective. My role was to simply assist him in the process.

Reluctant – putting it mildly – at first, Pepper soon warmed to the task and undertook it with his customary enthusiasm and – well – doggedness.

The one condition I put on the project was that I be permitted to add an occasional observation or comment along the way. With evident skepticism – and we all know how expressive a dog's face can be – Pepper agreed. So you will know who is speaking, my minor contributions are in italics, whereas Pepper's are in normal font.

The book was completed in 1992 under different conditions and for different purposes. The different conditions were we had moved to Philadelphia and Pepper's passing from a terminal illness diagnosed almost two years earlier. After his passing, it became very important for me to complete his book as he'd taken such joy in its writing. I also thought completing his book would be both a celebration of his life and also bring me a level of closure. Unexpectedly it also proved to be a needed catharsis.

I also wanted to share the journey Pepper and I had enjoyed with others in whose lives their pet companions were or are of equal importance and for those experiencing the recent loss of their beloved companions. My hope then, and now, is that our story will be of some comfort to others similarly blessed with comparable stories.

Why publish now, after all this time? There's a simple answer: I met someone whose feelings about pet companions are like my own and who happens to be a publisher. As I had before with other like-minded friends, I shared a copier store's version of Pepper's book. His response was immediate and direct, "I want to publish your book."

I hope Pepper is pleased and moved, and I hope you will be too.

Ron Wormser
Carmel, CA
March 2017

A Dog's Tale

<u>In the Beginning</u>

Big Apple Welcome

New York and I did not get off on the right paw, which is a little odd since in my case it had four chances. With all its problems, you would think that The Big Apple would surely have gone out of its way to make a favorable first impression. Not bloody likely.

I was born in Missouri, and was transported to New York City very much against my will at the exceedingly young age of about eight weeks. Happily, I have no recollection of the separation and subsequent trip east.

What I do recall with painful clarity is suddenly awakening in a small metal cage, in a room so brightly lit that it pained my tender young eyes, amid a great racket of yipping and yelping, surrounded by dozens of other equally miserable little creatures. In other words, I had landed in a pet store.

Even though I was quite small, my cage was not much larger and was made less so thanks to a wad of torn up newspapers pretending to be carpeting. It may be "All the News That's Fit to Print", but it surely wasn't fit for bedding.

Worse, it was impossible to sleep amid the constant din. I mean, the racket was unending.

As for food, periodically the cage door would be opened and a tiny bowl of gruel would be plopped down between the Obituaries and Business News.

If thirsty, I had to lick at a metal tube which, while so young as to be barely able to stand, even I knew wasn't the real thing.

When I felt the need to attend to certain other bodily functions, a rather frequent stirring in those early days, my only choice was to try to find a portion of the Business Section that wasn't doing double duty as bedroom or playpen.

At that age, it didn't mean much to me that I was able to do to Wall Street what some of its insiders had been doing to the rest of the country. It's not that I passed up the opportunity, it's just that I couldn't then appreciate its urinary, er, irony.

I learned later that these so-called living conditions are known in your world as solitary confinement, a particularly harsh form of punishment reserved for the worst offenders against society.

Why, then, I and so many others like me were given this form of hospitality as our introduction to New York City was and remains a cruel puzzle.

To make matters worse, for no apparent reason every day I would be removed from my small cell and placed in a larger one. But instead of more room, I was thrown in with many others.

Adding insult to injury, my new pen-mates were not my type. In fact, most often they were of very mixed and uncertain backgrounds. I mean, they weren't the sort I would have asked home for dinner, had I then had a home – and a dinner - to ask them to.

I guess this was our equivalent to your exercise yard, complete with both more space and more inmates, but still under intense supervision.

Talk about supervision! This larger cell was bordered on one side by a window while the other side opened onto a large room with lots of people milling about.

I soon learned that while I no longer had to endure the isolation of solitary confinement, I was now subject to group torture.

From the window side came a constant banging, while from the opposite side came a less frequent but more intense disruption as various two-legged animals approached then poked and prodded at us over the top of the cage.

As if all of that wasn't enough, my cell mates were busy either bouncing all over the place, nipping at anything and everything with razor-sharp tiny teeth, or redoing the flooring with equal fervor. And doing and doing and doing other crappy things I care not to describe.

As another form of specialized punishment, from time to time I would be hoisted out of the cage and placed within reach of a bawling two-year old whose high-pitched scream was paired with a wild, uncoordinated flailing of four limbs moving independently but each ultimately aimed at my very young, delicate nose.

That dangerous specimen would have in tow an older pair, a well-dressed couple, the female half of which would be making quite delightful and promising cooing sounds accompanied by cuddling motions.

Her pin-striped companion however was not having any of this 'make nice' routine. His contribution to this torture was to discourse, at great length, on my relative resale value, contrasting me with more preferable (i.e., profitable) investment opportunities promising a greater net return. He had obviously acquired considerable first-hand knowledge of dogs in his job on Wall Street.

These hazardous encounters would eventually cease - though not soon enough - and I would be rewarded with a prompt return to the collective cage. Which - by this time – was actually far preferable.

It was starting to dawn on me why New York does not enjoy an unvarnished reputation, instead giving the phrase 'home hospitality' a bad name. I was coming to understand why not everyone is thrilled with the prospect of moving here.

So I began to plot my escape. I had noticed that from time to time one of us would be removed from confinement and placed in a cardboard box after which he or she would depart the premises accompanied by one or more of folks like you, but only after a certain amount of paper-shuffling had taken place.

It's interesting to note the many rolls, er, roles that paper plays in my life, isn't it?

Of course, I had no idea what would happen once outside those noisy and irksome confines. But it seemed a good bet that it would be no worse and perhaps would be better than my existing circumstances. After all, what could be worse that spending my days trying to avoid damp, soiled newsprint and snapping teeth, and my nights confined to a small cell whose metal rungs were badly out of alignment with my rib cage, and being fed plastic food and metallic-tasting water?

So I began to study the behavior of those who were successful in their escapes to see if there were patterns which, if duplicated, would lead to my own liberation. But there seemed no consistency. A playful, cheery, indeed enthusiastic, demeanor might lead to freedom in one case, but not in another. Shyness and quiet dignity could lead to a cardboard carrying box - there's that ubiquitous paper again! - or it could land one back in the cage just as easily.

I grew frightened, absent a predictable means of gaining freedom: what could I do to hasten my own escape?

In time it simply happened. One day, this young -YES! - couple came in. While I can't tell you why, as soon as I saw them, I knew that they were going to be my way out. They appeared to know it, too. No sooner had we met and greeted each other than they seemed to want me as much as I knew I wanted them. Love at first sight!

After the requisite paperwork - this proved to be the last time that someone else attended to the paperwork; thereafter, it became my, 'er, responsibility - I, too, finally got placed into a cardboard Freedom Box.

Without a single glimpse backward, I left what had, after all, proven to be but a temporary 'home' and headed off for ----well, I didn't know for what, but I knew that with my new companions it would likely be wonderful. For the first time since arriving in Manhattan, I was happy; and New York no longer seemed quite so lonely and unwelcoming.

A pet store was, of course, not the brightest idea: convenient but exceptionally ill-advised. Had it not resulted in Pepper, it would have been monumentally stupid. These outlets for puppy farms are notoriously – and deservedly – of dubious quality. Anyone desiring a pet companion should only deal directly with reputable breeders. As splendid as Pepper is, he has been the exception that has proven the rule.

What's His Name?

It wasn't until I began this project in my ninth year that I encountered a question I'd never before had to consider: what do I call him?

While I have lived with him, slept with him, eaten his food, shared his joys and sorrows, played catch with him, romped with him on beaches and in parks, gone swimming with him – well, not really - , taken long walks in the woods and short trips to the doctors, stayed behind while he's gone to work for the day or abroad for weeks, through all the hills and valleys of our intimately shared existence, never before have I had the need to give him a name.

Of course he needed one for me right away. That's one of the ways we have arranged our lives together: he gets to do the name calling, and I get to bark at him. Seems to have worked just fine.

When I do need to get his attention, I have a range of verbal and non-verbal ploys which have gotten the job done. Of course some techniques work better in certain situations than others. For example, a simple unimaginative bark might do the trick, but not always. A painful whimper, on the other hand, always seems to work. A deep-throated angry growl gets a prompt response most of the time. Snorts and sneezes, however, are ignored unless done in rapid succession. A joyful whoop, usually prompted by a particularly exciting dream or the question, "Wanna go to the park?" – much more on that later - is one of my favorites.

Then there are non-verbal stratagems. If I really want to grab his attention, I'll use my teeth to grab the seat of his pants – and something more when he's done something deserving a bit more bite.

Putting my paw on his arm and looking at him fetchingly lets him know I want his attention, or more frequently, a lot more frequently, a taste of what he's eating.

So, although we've lived together quite successfully for more than nine years, this is the first time that I've had to figure out what to call him. I mean, if I'm going to be talking about him, I really should use something more personal than just "him".

Okay, so he needs a name. Fine. But what to call him if not 'him'?

Of course, I could use his given name. Since he calls me "Pepper", I could call him "Ron". But this obvious solution seems to me painfully conventional ......not unlike 'Pepper' if you want to know the truth. But let's not go there.

'Dad' seemed a possibility. But being biologically impossible, it just didn't seem right. What's more, it might encourage him to get even by calling me 'Dog'.

"It's The Dad and Dog Show!" Yuk.

It did, however, lead to another thought that seemed to suit both his species as well as our relative family relationship, 'The Old Man.'

I've heard him use it with great affection and respect with his own father. Since it is not only descriptive of our relationship, but also carries on a family tradition, I hope its use will please him as much as it does me.

So hereafter whenever talking about my human companion, I'll call him 'The Old Man', or just plain TOM.

What's Its Name?

Bonnie and I chose a breed and gender more easily than a name. We had quickly decided on a male miniature Schnauzer because we had fallen in love with a neighbor's in the small college town where we had lived before moving to New York.

That Schnauzer was called Mischief, and never was a dog more aptly named. Indeed his bright and mischievous nature is how we came to fall in love with the breed. If and when we were to want to add a dog to our family, it would be a male miniature Schnauzer.

But a few years later when we decided to start looking for one and started to consider names, we found ourselves confronted with all kinds of choices we hadn't considered: Did we want a 'doggy name' or a 'human name'? Fido or Frank? Should the name be short, crisp and businesslike; or should it have more than one syllable, the latter - so the theory went - making it easier for the dog to learn? Frank or Frankenstein?

Should we use a 'cute' name or one not intended – or likely – to make heads turn? Were we going to play the Manhattan game of being 'original', choosing a name that would presumably reflect well on ourselves, Manhattanites being competitive in everything? One that would immediately announce our creativity and with-it-ness or use a more mundane moniker and thus announce our dullness and mediocrity: Chaucer of Turtle Bay or Spot?

Should we use a typical Schnauzer name Fritz, Schnapps, or - my favorite - Whiskers - or strike out with a defiantly neutral one? Charlie?

In a burst of either diplomacy or cowardice – a distinction without a difference? - we ducked those prickly decisions and agreed to separately write down names which we simply liked for whatever reason and without having to explain why. No justifications, just possibilities.

Although I now have no recollection of any of Bonnie's or my own, I am certain of two things: we both had reasonably long lists, and Pepper wasn't on either.

Thus armed, off we set for the local pet store. As luck would have it, a male Schnauzer was available along with one or two females and other small breeds. The little male Schnauzer was alert and full of beans, a toy-sized Mischief.

A few minutes playing with him, and the decision was made. It's a fair question to ask who, in these circumstances, really decides: does the pet choose its companions, or the other way 'round?

So how did Pepper end up 'Pepper'?

The same way Jumbo ended up 'Jumbo'.

Ok. Who the hell is Jumbo?

Jumbo was a mutt my parents and I brought home from the vet shortly after having to put Lady to sleep when I was in high school. Lady was a beautiful black cocker spaniel that I had gotten three years earlier, after George, the dog I had spent 12 years growing up with, had died.

George was a pedigreed cocker given to my parents when both he and I were still wee lads. Literally. He was a few months old, small even in my 3 year old hands and had been christened "Late Date of Kay Crest" having come into this world somewhat behind schedule at Kay Crest Kennels. He had initially been acquired by the best friends of my parents who had 2 young daughters, both of whom proved to be allergic to the pup. Thus the gift to us.

Somewhere between Kay Crest and coming to our house he'd been unofficially tagged "George", and so he remained for the rest of his years.

His name unexpectedly led to a revelation about the elderly Scottish couple living next door. While they were with great affection known to all of us, parents and children, as 'Nanny' and 'Pummy', we soon learned that Pummy was a cover name for something a bit more dignified.

While we had always suspected this, the combination of their Scottish reserve and our southern respect for elders - this was, after all, West Virginia in the mid-'40's - had meant that the topic had never been broached. We may have been southern, but we weren't slow. We knew that Nanny and Pummy were unlikely Christian names, even for Scots.

We accidentally came into possession of his real name when George was first let loose from his basement jail into our fenced-in back yard. Left to roam free, George of course would wander wherever his puppy curiosity led him. That required my mother to stand on the back porch and in her atypically deep voice call out loudly, "George; here, George. George, come here!"

And from deep in the bowels of the neighboring garage where Pummy forever tinkered with his hoard of hardware store goodies being a retired drummer of such stuff came the obvious reply,

"Coming, Dear!"

Which wasn't the end to this back-yard dialogue. When it came my turn to be let loose in the back yard, Mom returned to the same porch and called to me about my choice for a sandwich. One of the options from time to time was caviar....the domestic A&P brand, to be sure. She'd call out, "Do you want caviar for lunch?" And from the garage next door would boom the reply, "Yes, Dear, and champagne, too!"

Anyway, after George came Lady, and I no longer recall how she came to have that name. But Jumbo's name? I recall that clearly.

Bringing him home from the vet in his box on the floor of the car, he jumped all over the place as puppies do, but with ears that hung out to here. Mom said something like, "Boy, he's quite a jumper."

I said, "Yeah, with ears like Dumbo the flying elephant."

Suddenly there it was: 'Jumbo'. A name that proved to be a perfect fit for that pup's personality.

And that's what happened with Pepper. We brought this little grey puppy home, placed him in his temporary prison, the back bath specially prepared for a puppy - wall-to-wall newspaper - and got down to the serious question of The Name.

There we were, armed with our respective lists, with all their possibilities. But once we started spending time with the little guy and getting to know his personality, none seemed to fit.

We'd try out a name for a day or so, but then conclude that it wouldn't be quite right. Some evenings we experimented with different possibilities, meaning that the puppy was called five or six different names in the space of an hour or two.

We figured, I hope correctly, that he was too young to be confused by our indecision. At that point, so far as we could tell, his interest was totally concentrated on processing foodstuffs in and out.

After several days, out of our frustration he became simply,

"Dog". Not when being referred to, as in, "Did you give the dog fresh water?" But rather, "Here, Dog, come here."

Picture it: a tiny puppy, sprawled on the carpet. Two grown adults down there as well. Both some distance from the little animal, each taking turns calling, "Dog. Here, Dog. Come here, Dog. "

I even tried, "Cat, here cat" once which Dog ignored but sadly not Bonnie who did respond. Firmly.

I don't know what the neighbors must have thought. Even I was beginning to feel just a bit silly. I can only imagine what Pepper must have been thinking. "How did I end up with these jerks? Take me back to the store!"

That actually led to considering "Dawg" as the permanent solution. For about 24 hours. That is, I was considering it. I think Bonnie was willing to humor me for a while, figuring anything was an improvement on 'Damnittohell' a dog name I'd long favored since childhood. The vision of using it on the streets of New York was almost irresistible, but not alas to you-know-who.

While memory plays tricks, it now seems to me that we went on like this for at least a week or more. Can you understand how really stupid and inept grown men and women can come to feel when after a week or so they can't come up with a name for a damned dog?! In short, we were getting desperate.

Heaven only knows what affect all these conflicting sounds were having on the poor puppy. I suspect that his pet store prison was looking pretty good next to the two babbling boobs he had come to live with.

Nor do I now recall which of us came up with the name that became his for life. But I do recall the moment very clearly. It was late. All three of us were exhausted, two of us from entertaining the third. We had assumed what had become our cusomary pre-bedtime positions in the hall just outside his room.

After a hard night's play, trying to keep up with the boundless energy of a puppy that had been cooped up all day, we were stretched out - spent, to be truthful - on the floor, backs against the wall in more ways than one, with the puppy that night in my lap about to be hoisted over the protective half-door into his cardboard bed.

Amid the exhausted silence, one of us piped up with, "How about 'Pepper"? As I said, I really don't know who had the idea. But once said, there it was, so perfectly obvious, and obviously perfect. Of course. Pepper. It fit him to a T. He looked like a Pepper. He acted like a Pepper. Heaven knows his personality was every bit like a Pepper. It was perfect. Pepper.

As the years have ticked by, it fits him just as much today as it did then.

Puppy Time

House- and Heartbreaking

I don't know why it's called 'housebreaking', since there's no known record of any actual breaking into houses. Perhaps it's because if all does not go well, it runs (!) the danger of actually breaking up a house. In my case, it nearly cost me my life.

Everything appeared normal at first. When I came home I performed my puppy-duties as a waste-processing machine dutifully, indeed happily. Food in one end and out the other. A function for which I was perfectly designed and in which I eagerly engaged.

My subsequent development again followed the normal trajectory: ever-increasing ability to perform where and when as instructed. There were of course occasional slip-ups about which I was as embarrassed as my human companions were unhappy. Nothing out of the ordinary.

Except for one thing. It is conventional wisdom that dogs do not wet where they sleep. But even after my training had in all other respects progressed very nicely, I began to spontaneously wet the bed. But that's not the worst of it.

By this time I was sleeping in their bed, and this little glitch was certainly not just my problem.

It was very strange. Days and evenings would pass without these wee hiccups. A last trip outside before bedtime and all would seem in order.

But, sometime during the night I would awaken to discover my bladder having just emptied in the very spot where I was stretched out. I hadn't stood up or otherwise moved from my prone position. But my hind legs and the sheeting underneath would be soaked. Obviously, while sound asleep, I had simply let go.

While not a nightly occurrence, it was not infrequent, happening several times a week. When it did, I would be taken outside, where naturally enough nothing more happened since it had all already happened. And of course the sheets would have to be changed. Then, after all this fussing, all of us would have to try to relax enough to return to sleep.

Worst of all, the problem persisted despite quite some time, months and months. In short, an unusual and distressing problem for all three of us. The concern, the really acute worry around me was palpable and grew more so in time.

At first, we thought Pepper's problem a physical one. We consulted our vet. He tested Pepper but could find nothing wrong. The problem continued. We tried another vet. Same results. We tried another, and another. No one could find a physiological reason for or explanation of the problem. We were given all kinds of remedies: different diets; controlling the amount of water taken in by limiting the amount in Pepper's water bowl; different schedules of walks, etc.

Then there were the medications: one type of pill after another. Nothing worked.

I should also report that Pepper seemed as surprised by his spontaneous bed-wetting as were we. The expression on Pepper's face was always one of befuddlement.

As the problem persisted, I shudder now to think of the added stress to which Pepper was subjected, the poking and prodding, the blood tests, the urine and stool samples whether provided voluntarily or drawn forcibly, the dietary changes, schedule variations, medications tried not to mention the disciplinary grief to which he was subjected.

As the matter dragged on, our capacity to respond calmly and rationally was steadily diminishing.

Several facts were becoming painfully clear. First, there was no detectable reason for Pepper's problem. This meant two things: (a) there was no dependable treatment; and (b) there was no reason to believe the problem would cease.

To say that this was an enormously stressful time in our lives is an understatement. In short, we were approaching our wits' end and the looming consequences of possible options were paralyzing.

The end of the story is equally strange as the problem itself.

After going from one vet to another, as a last resort we decided to try a major teaching and research pet hospital in New York called the Animal Medical Center. It is in all respects like any other teaching hospital where research and training as well as patient care take place. It is the sort of medical facility you and I would happily use. The only difference is that its patients are animals.

It was to this facility that we turned in one last, desperate try.

Their tests were even more exhaustive but just as inconclusive as all the others. Which is to say, quite conclusive: there was no identifiable cause for Pepper's behavior and thus no clear course of treatment. At that wrap-up meeting, the doctor then went on to say,

"Look folks, you clearly love your dog. But he has a problem the cause of which we cannot determine and therefore cannot treat. Nor can you continue to live your lives as you have. So you have to decide what you want to do. There are two basic choices: you can put Pepper to sleep, or you can try to find him another home where his problem will be less unacceptable than it has been for you. Perhaps a place in the country. But for his sake as well as for yours, you must do something. None of you can go on like this."

We gulped, of course, and swallowed that dry, hard one when your mouth is suddenly parched and your throat constricted. I think, I hope, we thanked that kind young man for all of his efforts and for his gentle though direct insistence that we face up to what we knew had been a looming and agonizing choice.

Slowly we began to discuss trying to find him another home. I don't recall discussing putting him to sleep. Certainly that fear was real but it remained unspoken. We clung to the perhaps unrealistic hope that we would be successful in finding an alternative home for him.

Now comes the unbelievable yet completely true denouement.

The simple and remarkable truth is that after that final night at the AMC, Pepper never again wet his - our - bed.

I know it's implausible. I know it seems contrived. I know it looks like a bending of fact to make a good story. But it happens to be true.

That's how this chapter in Pepper's life, and of our lives together, came to an end. Just as the cause of his problem could never be explained, neither could its cessation.

In a very real sense, after going through such a trying period and after facing the very real likelihood of losing him, we were in effect given another chance. He was given back to us, reborn in a way.

I think - I know - we hold him all the more dear as a result.

A Dog on Tiptoe

Did you ever see a dog tiptoe?

We've all seen dogs walk gingerly on ice, trying to maintain their traction. We've also seen them walk with great deliberation and care, approaching something strange or about which they don't feel confident. Or with the greatest of hesitation, slowly placing only one tentative paw out to test a strange surface or to head off in an uncertain direction. But actually tip-toe? Well, I swear Pepper did.

You see, when he came into our life and apartment, there was wall-to-wall carpeting. Apart from whatever had been on the floor where he was born, the metal rungs of the cage at the pet store, and the newspapers on the floor of his temporary quarters when he first came home with us, that carpeting had to be the first surface he really got to know.

Once he had the run of the apartment, and being a frisky pup he dashed everywhere, what was underfoot was carpet, except of course the kitchen. There were even rugs in the bathrooms.

Since he was only in the kitchen to eat and drink, I rather doubt he was too focused on what was beneath his feet as distinct from his mouth.

Otherwise wherever he went, he had carpeting on which to walk, run, romp, roll, play, and sleep. As a puppy maturing into a young dog, that's what he knew. Whatever surfaces he encountered outside the apartment, once inside there was always something underfoot that ensured firm and reliable footing.

However there came a time when the wall-to-wall was replaced with area carpets bordered by expanses of brightly polished, newly-polyurethaned, gorgeous dark oak parquet flooring. Very handsome...and very slippery.

Well, it didn't take long for this robust Schnauzer to discover, to his great surprise, discomfort and embarrassment, the change. At first whenever not on the carpet, he was completely befuddled, since even standing still - much less moving about - was suddenly an uncertain and therefore unsettling experience.

Early on, spills were frequent, with Pepper splayed out with each leg in a different direction or flat on his side. Experiencing this for the first time, Pepper became exceedingly cautious in his movements, which is when I swear I saw him actually tip-toeing around the place, trying to get the hang of it.

Whereas he had been able to reliably bolt, dart, run, and romp without a second thought, now even a stately walk was fraught with uncertainty, and anything more enthusiastic was downright dangerous. Even getting started was slippery business, making the poor thing look remarkably like the Roadrunner, rear wheels spinning furiously before there would be any traction followed by forward movement.

Hard as getting going was, stopping was nearly impossible. At first all four legs would become rigid, with the toes looking for something to dig into while the rapidly advancing object - table, chair, wall - loomed ever closer, at which point the rear legs began backpedaling madly, causing the forward slide to begin to slow at last.

Eventually Pepper became quite expert in judging these slides, like an experienced base-stealer in the major leagues. You could almost see him measuring it out in his head, computing the distance and velocity, timing his run arid then applying the braking action so that the inevitable skid didn't end in a smashed nose and pride.

Straight lines were relatively easy.

Slowing to turn corners proved more complex, since simple slowing and stopping was only the first part. There was the turn to be navigated and either he could get underway again or he might have to make yet another turn. Since rooms in the apartment opened off of a main hallway, moving from one to another almost always meant having to manage at least one and usually two 90-degree maneuvers.

Pepper had to work it out so that both his front and rear made it around the corner, rather than having the front make it into the room while his rear was still heading down the hall. Make the wrong calculation and the reward was a sharp and painful encounter by his ribs with the door jam.

NASA has computers to manage lunar launches, orbits and trajectories. Pepper had to rely on his own wits to work out equally complex equations. Eventually, through painful trial and error, he got it all figured out, of course. And in relatively short order, he was back to his frisky self, running and romping all over the place, having in the meantime added complex slipping and sliding to his repertoire.

But every now and then, usually in an energetic burst prompted by exceptional excitement, he'd fail to or forget to recompute and - splat – either a rump on the floor or ribs into a door jam. Never slowed him down, though. Got right back up and kept chargin'.

Tricks of the Trade

Very early on in our lives together, usually after we have mastered what you so misleadingly call 'housebreaking', you begin a strange but persistent endeavor to teach us what you call 'tricks'.

Well, let me teach you a thing or two about this subject.

First and foremost what to you is a trick, to us is a tedious chore to master simply to get a meager morsel of, get this, 'reward'. It is food damn it – pure and simple.

Worse, your tricks are boring. I mean, really boring. After all: Sit? Stay? Roll over? Play dead? Shake hands? Dull, dull, dull. No prize for imagination or creativity here.

Considering what we are capable of learning and doing as so-called working dogs assisting some of you in your daily lives, herding cattle or sheep, detecting drugs or other substances to keep you safe…..given our capabilities, how do you think we feel when all you want to teach us is to sit, stay and roll over?!?

Stop and think about it from our perspective. Just how exciting do you think shaking hands is to a dog? When was the last time you saw us greet each other by shaking each other's paws?

The point is: Why do you insist on trying to get us to mimic your behavior? I don't see you copying ours. Not that I wouldn't truly love to see you meet a friend on the street and immediately start sniffing each other's tail.

And 'sit'? Spoiler alert: We already know how to sit! We also know how to run, jump, roll over and a bunch of other things that come naturally to us. That's part of who we are, of what we do. It's baked into our DNA.

Want to know the ugly truth: you aren't teaching us anything we don't already know. What you are trying to get us to do is to perform and to perform on your demand. It's a control thing.

Want to know the beautiful truth: we let you play this game out of our deep sense of compassion and reciprocity. You give us a home, you feed and care for us, you keep us warm and safe and you make us feel not just wanted but loved. The least we can do in return is to perform even silly tricks if and when asked. Besides, it seems to please you so much!

But a little more imagination and challenge would certainly be appreciated.

Grandpaw's Trick

TOM's father - should he be called TOM's TOM? - visits us twice a year. He's a kindly old gent in his 80's, still enjoying reasonably good physical and mental health. A plain man with simple tastes and interests, he is a joy to have as company while TOM is at work.

Grand-TOM and I curl up in a lounge chair and have contests to see who can get in the most naps before TOM returns to disturb our slumbers. True, there is an occasional dispute over who gets in the chair first; and I make no concession to his age. But generally, I enjoy having him around.

This generosity of spirit on my part is because of the evident affection and respect between TOM and his father. It is obvious even to me that there is a deep bond between them. Listening as I occasionally do to their conversations, feeling the atmosphere when they are together, I can just tell that there is a loving closeness. As part of the family, I naturally want to do my share to contribute to this all-round good feeling.

So during these twice-yearly week-long visits, I don't raise – or cause - a stink when TOM and I are relegated to the den for sleeping accommodations. TOM gives his father the master bedroom with my double bed and electric blanket, an arrangement about which I am never consulted and which is not at all to my liking. But, as I said, I struggle mightily to be a pleasant go-along member of the family.

For seven long nights twice a year, I have to make do sharing a narrow, worn-out sofa, TOM being too lazy to open it into the sofa-bed it actually is. I worry constantly whether I'll roll over and end up on the floor, or TOM will and I will end up as puppy mush.

The annual Christmas visit produces particularly uncomfortable nights since I must make do without the soothing warmth of my electric blanket. You've heard of 'three dog nights'? Well, our version is two-people nights.

The fact is, despite being somewhat under-rested, I greatly enjoy the added company and attention.

However, there can be less positive features to these paternal visits. For example, I have been completely unable to crack Grand-TOM's obstinate refusal to share any of his food with me. Unlike his son who always sees to it that I get a sampling of what he is eating, the father's resistance to my most persistent and endearing entreaties is damnably unshakable. I can certainly see where TOM got his legendary stubbornness. The acorn didn't fall very far from that tree, I can tell you.

And he's not above trying to induce me to perform various acts of absurd behavior, aka tricks. His favorite is bending over, rump facing me, putting his clasped hands a foot off the floor and imploring me to jump through his hoop.

Between learning about stubbornness from the two TOMs and my German heritage, I am perfectly capable of being stubborn with the best of you.

Here's the deal: no food, no jumping through hoops. And get that rump out of my face!

Frustrated by his own efforts to teach me his trick – aka bloody stupid chore – later that night he offered some advice to TOM when he was trying for the umpteenth time to teach me to shake hands.

Perhaps nursing residual stubbornness from the hoop jumping incident, I was in no mood to be cooperative.

During a paws, 'er pause, Grand-TOM took TOM aside – thinking I wouldn't hear but of course I did – and carefully and caringly said, "Son, don't you know, a dog can't understand, 'shake hands'? You have to say, 'Give me your paw.'"

Can We Talk?

There's another trick you try mightily to get us to perform, to speak.

Many of you seem to think it is possible – even desirable - for us to speak. You literally beg us to do so.

While only one trick among many, it's certainly the one that makes the least sense to us. And you know how keen our senses are, right?

Why you persist in the illusion we can speak makes us dog-gone nuts, or at least those of us who still have them.

Just for a moment, let's pretend that one day one of us will become parrot-like and be able to repeat what is heard, including all those lovely curses you exchange with each other from time to time. Or will recite the Gettysburg Address after listening to your kid memorize it for school.

Have you ever stopped to think what we might actually say? Remember, we see and hear all. How would you like to hear your cuddly canine companion already comfortable in your shared bed look up as you disrobe and scream at the top of its lungs, "Sweet Jesus, put it back on!"

Or while entertaining your best, closest friends your furry friend wanders into the room, stops, dutifully sits as trained, wags tail beguilingly and blurts out, "Hey folks, wanna know what I saw them do last night?!"

No, I really don't think you want us to speak.

One of the reasons, perhaps one of the strongest reasons, we have become your best friends is that we don't kiss and tell.

You know that and rely on us to be completely and totally discreet, to keep our mouths shut.

We see and hear things that you wouldn't dream of entrusting to anyone else. You feel completely at ease saying, doing, sharing anything with us. You trust us absolutely secure in the knowledge that we won't talk.

If we did speak, it would almost certainly end our very special relationship with each other. And I don't think either of us wants that to ever happen.

Picking Pepper's Pocket:
A Cut Below

*Since it had never been our intention to breed Pepper, the plan
had always been to have him neutered. There were two reasons
for this. First, I felt it would remove a source of frustration for
him, and also, according to then-prevailing medical opinion,
contribute to his general health and well-being. Secondly, it
would also remove a cause of humiliation to me.*

*There are few things about living with a male dog that are more
embarrassing than having him hump whatever strikes his fancy:
towels, pillows, your arms and legs, and especially the arms and
legs of your guests.*

*I think it was Mark Twain who observed that, "Man is the only
animal that blushes, or needs to." Well, in the absence of a willing female, a young, vigorous male canine with lust in his heart
and hormones in his veins can prove problematic. Blushing is
the least of it.*

*You may recognize the symptoms if you have a male teenager in
the house.*

*Besides, have you even seen a dog actually enjoy this ersatz ex-
perience? Sure, they start off with great enthusiasm. But I don't
remember ever seeing a satisfactory conclusion. They invariably
seem to, well, peter out.*

*I can't recall any dog looking other than disconsolate and slink-
ing away from the object of his ardor. And that's if matters are
left to run their course. If interrupted 'er prematurely, your
otherwise friendly companion can become positively dogged,
eager to pursue his passion while you are just as eager to
enforce coitus interruptus.*

*It's not a gratifying experience for either of you. And who can
blame him? After all, how would you feel, the roles being reversed?*

*No, unless there are powerful reasons to the contrary, surely
neutering is the easier, more humane, wiser course for all*

parties.

To my surprise, and perhaps to his, for some time after being neutered, Pepper would on rare occasions start humping my leg or arm.

I'd immediately look at him in surprise. Not too long into his activity, he would pause, get this perplexed look on his face and, avoiding my eyes, dispiritedly go somewhere not too far away and lay down, resting his head between his front paws and look up at me with what I swear were the saddest eyes I'd ever seen.

Talk about a guilt-trip......

Patience

When I was young, maybe 2 or 3, I went through a prolonged period when something was amiss with my digestive system. Not to be unnecessarily graphic, but the evidence appeared in my stools and indicated, according to the docs, an incomplete processing of certain nutritional materials. Since the symptoms first appeared not long after I graduated from Puppy Chow to Adult Food, TOM figured that the first pass at corrective action should be a change in my diet.

TOM would introduce a new entrée and/or a new manufacturer for several days, in theory long enough to permit my system to adjust to the new product and to determine if it would have any beneficial effect.

This became a kind of culinary roulette, but we were looking more for a magic cork than a bullet.

Happily I can report that these changes had no adverse effect on my hearty appetite. I ate as greedily as ever.

While this rotation did not resolve my problem, it did afford me the chance to sample quite a variety of commercially prepared dog food. This topic is worthy of its own seasoning, er, treatment; food for further thought, as it were. The chapter "Canine Cuisine", appearing later in these pages will fill you in on this topic nearly as much as it did me.

But I digest....

After testing the diagnostic competence of an array of vets - and the depths of TOM's wallet -, it was finally determined that the cause of my problem was a malfunctioning pancreas. Apparently it was failing to produce whatever it normally does to break down the fat content in food. My mis-behaving pancreas was thus preventing proper digestion.

Happily this was neither serious nor all that difficult to treat. All that was required was a specially prepared commercially available low-fat diet supplemented with medication.

When you are required to go on a bland diet, you cringe and have nightmares of piles upon piles of pasta, an Endless Noodle. In my case, however, I lucked out. My diet was to be changed to a canned chicken-and-rice mixture manufactured by a company whose specialty is the preparation of medically supervised animal diets available only through vets' offices.

While this may not sound like a five-star menu to you, when contrasted with the usual mixture of animal wastes and chemicals that passes for normal dog food – see that Chapter I mentioned above coming later - I had landed in hog-heaven, so to speak.

But there's no free lunch - or dinner - for dogs, either. There was a price to be paid for this good fortune. To the lovely chicken and-rice was to be sprinkled on and then stirred in a medicine that would begin the process of breaking down the limited fat content, thereby doing chemically what my malfunctioning pancreas could not do.

Since the medicinal powder was both odorless and tasteless, there shouldn't have been any problem, right?

Wrong!

I'll tell you what the problem was. The mixture of food and medicine had to sit for 20 minutes before it could be served! This interregnum was to provide time for the chemical to do its work before I could wolf down the grub.

Now, put yourself in my paws. You are limited to only one meal a day, and it is served up only after you've had the full day to dream about it. Imagine the anticipation!

The time finally comes. You hear the fridge open, the can opener whir, the heavenly sounds of fork clanging onto bowl....and the smell, the wonderful fragrance of nourishment and joy wafting its way to your face, up your exceptionally well-equipped, finely honed nose and into the pit of your stomach. What digestive juices you do produce begin their run.

And then you have to wait 20 minutes!! Worse, that's 20 of your minutes which means it's over 2 hours in my time. 2 HOURS!!

Try it yourself. Fast all day. Come home tired and hungry. Prepare your favorite meal. Sit it on the table and yourself across the room. See it. Smell it. And then try not to move a muscle for 20 minutes.

Further, imagine having to do this every day. Dog-gone cruel! Canine water-boarding!!

At this point, Pepper and I were living alone as Bonnie and I had separated and subsequently divorced.

Pepper had to endure this routine for several years. No doubt to his great relief, and, frankly, mine as well, eventually he was slowly and successfully weaned off the medication, though he has remained on the canned chicken-and-rice diet ever since.

He has described the dreadful testing of his character that he faced nightly. The only missing element - other than that absent enzyme - which should be added is the conclusion to this ritual.

I would arrive home at 7. After the necessary business was concluded outside, I would first prepare Pepper's dinner; set the timer on the stove; and then during the 20 minute interval, prepare my own meal. After the required interval, the timer would go off; I would put Pepper's bowl on the floor and set about finishing my own dinner's preparations. He would finish his with his customary dispatch, and then the two of us would adjourn to the den and TV news. Sounds dull, 'eh?

Not quite. When that buzzer sounded, you didn't want to be caught between where Pepper had been waiting and his bowl. In a tiny Manhattan kitchen, care had to be taken. I mean, once that timer went off, 15 pounds of crazed animal moved. And I do mean moved!

Getting in his way would not have been sane or safe.

Daily Routine

The Daily Drill

Back in the days when TOM had a job, we had developed a set routine, a daily schedule that even now we pretty much follow.

We did this for two reasons: first, as you know, we dogs strongly prefer established routines. We have enough to cope with, living in your world rather than our own; so a regular schedule minimizes our daily stress.

The other reason is that fortunately, TOM seems to be of like nature. After studied observation, I came to the belief that it was his way of accomplishing all he wanted to get done every day. Or maybe he was just being smart: he must have realized it was clearly better and easier to do things my way.

I say a "regular routine", but that misrepresents the matter somewhat. Since TOM's job necessitated a goodly amount of travel, in truth we had two routines, one when he was in residence and one when he wasn't.

The in-residence schedule went like this.

5:45 a.m. Reveille! Six feet on the floor. TOM uses a two-pronged attack to start the day, one a loud and irritating alarm clock and music from a clock radio. I don't know why he uses two. The dastardly duo began not long after he started to travel a great deal. Maybe it was the confusion from always being in a different time zone. Or maybe it was chronic fatigue. Or maybe it was his way of ensuring I'd awaken. Whatever the reason, neither of us ever, ever overslept. 'Though I certainly tried my darnedest more than once......

Pepper's guesses as to my reasons for two alarms are close to the truth. I've never been a morning person and have always had difficulty awakening and getting underway.

When Pepper came to live with us, Bonnie being more of a morning person was the obvious choice for taking Pepper out in the morning whereas I, always having been an evening person, was the obvious candidate for the last walk at night.

So when Bonnie and I separated, when folks asked me what the biggest adjustment was, I was only half-joking when I said, "Getting up to walk Pepper first thing in the morning."

Thus brought crashing into consciousness, since I am already dressed - except for the coldest of winter days when even I consent to wearing a sweater - I can catch another 'Z' or two while TOM puts on enough gear to face the world without fear of attack, arrest or frostbite.

After a quick trip to his own sandbox and after putting water on to boil for his morning tea, out into the world we go, one of us literally. Mind you, the purpose of this excursion at such an unseemly hour is solely to attend to certain bodily functions and definitely not for a scenic tour of Early Manhattan.

While we're all business at that hour, even then we must be mindful to avoid both early joggers and the private garbage collectors both in full stride and quite intent.

As soon as my duty is done, it's upstairs and back to bed for a short snooze for me while TOM goes about his stretching, shaving and dressing routine. It's one of my most favorite parts of the day: a nap having the still-warm bed all to myself!

8:00 a.m. Breakfast! Chow! Grub! FOOD! Mine isn't much to get excited about, being just a few, a very few small chunks of my canned diet. Not since my earliest puppy days have I enjoyed a really proper breakfast.

But TOM as always is too polite to eat in front of me without sharing at least a few snippets of his meal. While he breakfasts watching the news of the day, I am watching him move fork or spoon from plate to mouth and from mouth to plate, over and over again. I guess there's something about watching live action that stimulates the appetite. It certainly does mine!

Thankfully, frequently – but not nearly enough – TOM will interrupt his cycle by extending his hand with a morsel of his food for me.

Being of polite nature myself, I return his kindness by always being demonstrably delighted with whatever morsel comes my way.

Know what I've discovered? His food always, well almost always tastes much better than my own.

So much so that when he seems to have temporarily forgotten about sharing, I'll give him a gentle reminder by lightly tapping his arm with my paw. Only rarely has that not been sufficient to restart the sharing.

To spare us both the embarrassment I will refrain from describing the rare exceptions and their consequences, other than to say they have been successful for me. To the victor belong the morsels!!

8:30 a.m. Downstairs for a quick trip to the neighborhood bakery. While TOM gets the evening's bread, I help clean up the leftovers from everyone else's morning muffins. En route, naturally I check out a few of the trees, parking meters and walls, attending to such personal matters as may be needed.

8:45 a.m. Definitely not my favorite part of the day. After a farewell hug and kiss, and any last minute instructions - always including a superfluous, "Be a good boy today" off TOM goes while I am left behind to fend for myself.

It's odd, these daily partings. Despite their frequency, they never get any easier. After all these years, I still hate to see him close that door! Tender as his goodbyes are, it still hurts every day.

It's no easier for me. Five days a week, every week, every year. Still, it's a daily ache. After coming back upstairs from his last walk before I go to work, he'll jump up into his favorite chair or spot on the sofa and then sit there, looking at me with an expression that never fails to melt my heart. After a farewell hug and kiss, I lift myself, if not my heart, towards the door and turn for a last look and that "Be a good boy today" farewell. He's still sitting and still looking with that same soulful expression. Boy, it hurts. Every day.

7:30 p.m. A key in the lock, the door opens and there he is at last. HAPPINESS!! JOY!!!

A one-time significant other who was in residence and would arrive home earlier, after observing this scene for a while she announced loudly as TOM entered the apartment, "God's Home!"

Nonetheless, the first order of business is business. Mine is to promptly be leashed, anxiously await the arrival of the elevator and then taken right outside so that various pressing matters can be attended to.

This excursion is as brief as circumstances permit, meaning that once my duty is done, we can promptly return upstairs for what's really important: DINNER.

Now for you, dinner is probably nothing special. Just another task with three distinct steps: preparation, consumption and clean-up. A chore, a drudge, a bridge between the hectic day and a couch-potato evening.

Well, dinner ain't at all like that for me. It happens to be my only real meal of the day. My hunch would be that if you were limited to only one feeding in each 24-hour period, you too would be a bit more attentive to this daily ritual.

TOM, being TOM, is very sensitive about this. He prepares and gives me my dinner before or while preparing his own. Of course, he no doubt understands that if he didn't have his priorities sorted out in quite this fashion, he might find it a little awkward moving about the kitchen with my teeth planted firmly in his ankle, or higher.

Once I've finished my dinner and TOM's is ready, we retire to the den and repeat the same drill as at breakfast: he watches the news and I watch him while we both consume his meal, what is for me a delicious dessert course.

8:30 p.m. With nourishment now on board, fueled up and ready to go, it is time for our one serious outing during the work week. Off we go for our evening excursion around the neighborhood, mostly keeping to one of two set itineraries: one to the north and one to the south. This mile or so hike is a real delight, as it gives me a chance to check up on the day's happenings in the area, getting the scent so to speak of what is new and different. Since we follow pretty much the same routes, I have evolved certain way stations over the years that require my nightly attention. This is not unlike the time-clocks that watchmen must stop at on their nightly rounds, both of us punching in in our own way.

This is also the time when, most nights, we attend to the serious business of grocery shopping. The frequency is necessitated by the reality of one of TOM's hands is occupied holding my leash, leaving only the one other to tote that barge or lift that bale.

There is yet another purpose served by these nightly hikes. They are an excellent indicator of TOM's mood and of the type of day he has had. If our pace is leisurely and if I am given free rein to scout and sniff at an unhurried pace, it's a safe bet that his day was a good one. On the other hand, if we rush along and if I am pulled and tugged away from following my nose for news, I know that it's probably not the night to ask for an increase in my allowance.

9:15 p.m. The walk being over, it is time to settle down for the surprises in the evening's briefcase, after first finding our respective places in our shared easy chair.

This triggers the nightly game: who gets into the chair first? Not that in the end it makes any difference, since I always end up stretched out along his thigh with my back and neck and ears within easy and constant reach. But if I get there first, I tease him by stretching out the width of the seat, letting him figure out where there's room for his much larger self. But if he's managed to settle in ahead of me, my assigned spot is reserved and it does no good to try to plop down any other place.

Once arranged in our assigned seats, while TOM attends to his stack of papers, I stretch out next to him. Since the papers sometimes seem to get him irritated, it's my job to soothe him down. Making sure that certain parts of my body are within easy reach seems to do the trick.

It is a curious thing, that. TOM can be completely absorbed in his work, even to the point of discontinuing the stroking. There is no verbal communication between us, nor any physical interaction other than my being snuggled up next to him. Simply being with him in this quiet way, all seems right with the world.

A view I share.

11:00 p m Last trip to the streets for what TOM refers to as "emptying the tanks." While certainly serving that purpose, it also gives TOM a chance to stretch his legs and clear his lungs, if not his mind, from the rigors of the past couple of hours. Just as he wants me to empty a certain body organ, I'm certain he's trying to achieve the same result with a different organ.

11:30 p.m. Now comes my least favorite part of the day, the nightly grooming. This ordeal is so unpleasant that it deserves to be relegated to its own chapter. See "A Groom With A View."

Midnight: After my nightly torture, one of the best parts of the day happily follows. While TOM reads his newspaper - ever thoughtful, I let him use the paper first - he treats himself to a snack. And as is his custom, he shares small portions with me. While he's trying to make sense of the day's news, I'm concentrating on scents of another kind. You might say I have a nose for news! But then again, you might not. He's nourishing his mind, whereas I'm nourishing my whole body.

1 a.m.: The day is done. Into the sack we go. I curl up in his crook, rest my head on his arm and stretch out against his chest. In our spoon position, TOM will whisper some final thoughts on the day past or the one ahead, and always some endearment about how he feels about me and our life together.

As we drift off, warm and secure, me wrapped in his arms, all I can do is heave a deep, grateful sigh and think how far I have come from that small metal cage in that pet store. Not a night goes by that I don't think how truly lucky I am, and how lucky we are that we have each other.

As close as Pepper and I are, as much as we share, there's a special quality of tenderness in our goodnights. It seems to happen every night. We'll have arranged ourselves in our customary positions, just as Pepper has described it: he in my crook, the two of us in a spoon-like arrangement. As I whisper an endearment or two, I wiggle even closer. And he does, too. It's as if we can't get close enough. Which, as I think about it, is just about how I feel; and I gather, how he feels, too.

Canine Cuisine

It's Not Nice to Mess With Mother Nature

Clearly you have forgotten that back when we were first evolving into our respective species, we all had before us the same sources of nourishment. All of us land-based creatures had to live off the same land.

There were no species-specific aisles: one for you and another one for us.

So when and why and who decided that while you got to continue to live off the land, we had to begin living off the laboratory?

I'll tell you who: NOT US!

Just because you started taking us into your caves for companionship and further 'domestication', what gave you the right to start tinkering with our diet? When and why did you decide that what had been our traditional nourishment was no longer appropriate or sufficient?

Why, WHY substitute chemicals for real food? Us! Your so-called best friends? And why do you persist in perpetuating this preposterous punishment? Treating us like, well, dogs?!?!?!?!

OUTRAGEOUS!!

Despite thousands of years of so-called evolution, decades of being fed the drivel you've manufactured, try putting down a piece of fresh meat in one bowl and a spoonful of your chemicals in another and see which one your best friend chooses.

The point is that despite all your best and perhaps even well-intended efforts and vast sums researching and coming up with a constantly changing supply of chemically-laced dog food, given a choice we'd opt for our original diet every time.

You constantly observe us lusting after a piece of your lamb chop, happily gnawing away on a bone or bone-flavored chew, a drip of ice-cream on the pavement, peanut butter on your finger, grabbing stray pieces of cheese within our reach, yet you punish us for following our instincts and give us gruel instead of real food.

Want to know why we're always hungry? Always begging for something to eat?

Doesn't it ever occur to you that what you call 'being bad' is simply us being us seeking to satisfy our basic natures?

Stop and ask yourselves: Is this denial of nature and an enforced artificial chemical diet truly for our benefit, or for yours?

Not yet convinced?

Read on.

You Call This Food?!

It's about time we sat down, not for a meal, but for a heartburn-to-heartburn talk about what you give us to eat.

That we have a keen interest in food probably comes as news to you since you act as if you don't think we care much about the subject. Why do we say that?

To begin with, most of you only feed us once a day.

Then you give us the same meal every day of our lives.

This disregard for our palates is compounded by what you give us to drink. Our liquid refreshment is usually limited to ordinary tap water. And that, very often, has been left sitting around all day.

Not the hi-fallutin' bottled variety for us, with or without gas, fresh from the fridge. No, indeed. While you are quenching your thirsts with chilled fancy stuff imported from great distances, we are treated, if that's the right word, to the tepid local variety.

What is unclear about this - in addition to the water itself of course - is that if the stuff out of the tap isn't good enough for you, why do you give it to us?

If you think this outpouring about our water is a pipe dream, why don't you take some of your own medicine? Try treating yourself to what you give us. Pour yourself a glass from the tap; let it sit all day at room temperature; go for a long walk; and then see what it tastes like to you at the end of the day.

So after starving us all day and giving us stale tap water to drink, when you do get around to putting some food in front of us, what do you do? You give us the same ol' crap, day in and day out. Night after boring, dull, unimaginative night.

I ask you, is this any way to treat your beloved pet companions? And if that's how you treat –some treat! - your best friends, what in heaven's name do you do to your worst enemies?

Of course we are our own worst enemies. Famished and weak from hunger, we gulp down what you laughingly call 'dinner', fearful that you'll even take this gruel away if we don't evidence adequate enthusiasm. Starvation is, after all, a terrific motivator.

Seeing our apparent enthusiasm, you conclude that we're not only satisfied but seemingly happy with what you've dished out for us.

Then you have the audacity to snap at us if we evidence the slightest interest in what you are eating! You firmly instruct us not to beg, and banish us if we don't stop pleading for the tiniest morsel of edible food.

Just once we'd like to turn the table on you. Literally.

Here's what I mean. Take a look at the contents from one among the multitude of choices of what to feed Fido at your local grocery store:

"Water sufficient for processing. Chicken, Poultry By-Products, Soy Flour, Vegetable Gums, Salt, Potassium Chloride, Iron Oxide, Methionine Supplement, Sodium Nitrate (To Promote Color Retention), Zinc Oxide, Ferrous Sulfate, Vitamin E Supplement, Choline Chloride, Manganous Oxide, Copper Oxide, Vitamin A Supplement, D-Calcium Pantothenate, Thiamin Mononitrate, Vitamin Supplements (D-3, B-12.)"

How appetizing does that sound to you? Yet you happily lay it before us and call it "dinner". What the bloody hell is goin' on here?!

But wait, there's more good news. Elsewhere on the label it is noted that the moisture content is a maximum of 78%, leaving a minimum of 22 % for the rest of the goodies. In other words, if I've got this right, what you're really giving us is about 1/5 chemicals and 4/5 stale water!

Sound appetizing to you? Are you licking your lips? Do you think this array of chemicals sitting in water which has sat in the warehouse and then on the shelf for who-knows-how-long and is then pushed under our noses once a day adequately reflects your love and devotion to our care and well-being?

Doesn't it bother you that most of what goes into our food is banned by law from yours?

Hasn't it ever struck you as odd that millions and probably billions of dollars have been spent on coming up with a product you calmly put before us but which you won't dare touch yourselves?

Therein, dear reader, lies the heart, or stomach of the problem: Those who buy it don't eat it.

The Affirmative Action Glutton

Pepper is the world's least fussy eater. He has always had a healthy, vigorous appetite. He consumes a meal faster than any animal I've ever seen. A real affirmative action glutton. Gulps anything and everything down with equal abandon.

His regular dog food. Morsels of anything I am eating: fruit, veggies, chicken, fish, a rare lamb chop and rarer piece of beef, cookies, popcorn, peanuts – whatever I offer, he gobbles down and waits impatiently for more.

In fact, in all the years we have lived together I've only seen him walk away from one thing.

While Bonnie and I were still together, we'd occasionally lie on the floor watching television. She'd have her regular Coke next to her and my Diet Coke was next to me. I had tried to get her to try the Diet Coke, but one sip was more than enough. Never again. And, wives being wives, I would occasionally be treated to, "How can you drink that awful stuff?!"

Well, the first time we were so arranged after Pepper came to live with us, he'd eagerly slurp down as much of Bonnie's Coke as he could. But every time I offered my Diet Coke, he'd take one sniff and walk away.

You know what came next: "See, not even Pepper will drink that stuff."

Betrayed by the little bastard!

Repainting the Kitchen

At one point in his youth, Pepper developed some type of gastro-intestinal disorder. After checking him out, the vet didn't think it was anything too serious, thankfully. But I was instructed to give Pepper a dose of medication that looked suspiciously like Pepto-Bismol twice a day.

To affect its administration and ensure its consumption, I was given a syringe and told to fill it with the prescribed amount of medicine, put one hand around Pepper's muzzle, thereby keeping his mouth closed, place the end of the syringe in his mouth be-tween his teeth and jowl, and use the plunger to insert the medi-cation into the back of his mouth. With his mouth held closed, he would instinctively swallow the stuff. So the vet said.

Sounded easy enough in the doctor's office. But the vet didn't think to tell me, nor did it occur to me to ask, what I should do in the event Pepper didn't feel like playing the prescribed game. I didn't inquire since Pepper has always been an easy patient. When it comes to giving him pills, he's quite relaxed about let-ting me pop open his mouth, shove a pill in at the back, and then hold his muzzle closed while he swallows. So I figured that the Pepto-Bismol wasn't going to be a big deal either.

Wrong! I don't know whether it was the taste of the stuff or the means of its administration or both, but Pepper was having no part of either.

At first I tried doing it while Pepper was on the floor, thinking that is where he would feel most comfortable and secure. Getting my hand around his muzzle and the syringe inserted were easy enough. But once the first drop of pink ooze hit his chops, off he went. Violently. Yanking his head away. Trying desperately to shake my hand off his muzzle. Pulling, tugging, resisting to beat all hell, and more often than not escaping while I had a near-full syringe in my hand.

Not to be outsmarted by a mere 14 pound dog, I next began to attempt the deed with Pepper on a counter in the kitchen, relying on the height and confined area to restrict his resistance. Not a whit. Changing the site didn't alter his reaction one iota. He still didn't like it and resisted just as furiously except that his escape was cut off.

Well, all I can tell you is that while Pepper eventually recovered, for weeks I had pink polka-dots all over the kitchen.

The Streets of New York

Getting Mugged

Among the early lessons I had to learn growing up in Manhattan was how to prepare myself for the physical assaults to which I was being subjected from presumably well-intentioned but misguided strangers. And it wasn't just me, but most every canine, German shepherds and pit bulls being the exceptions.

It happens all the time. I'm strolling down the street, minding – and doing - my own business when out of the blue, some character places himself or herself squarely in my path, reaches down, and either pounds my head or pulls my ears.

For starters: Why do you bipeds think pounding on my noggin' and tuggin' on my lobes are friendly gestures and pleasurable experiences?

I've observed how you greet each other and it ain't anywhere close to how you greet me. If you do greet someone on the street – admittedly not a frequent occurrence in New York – it looks to me quite warm and friendly. But your manner of greeting me is both aggressive and painful. Why?!?!?

You don't greet us the same way you greet each other and you don't see us greet each other the way you greet us. So what's with the head pounding and ear tugging?!?!?!?!

Sure, once in a while an overly enthusiastic puppy may think tugging on ears is the cat's meow but if you'll notice, the subject of this attention doesn't often share in the enthusiasm.

Unwanted as both the head and ear assaults are, often they are only the first of two painful blows delivered almost always by women. After the head pounding and ear tugging, another one arrives, this one to my nose.

How does this happen? Watch for it the next time you're working, 'er walking the streets. A lady bends down to administer the first two wallops to the head and ear of some unsuspecting pup. What happens next? Right. A heavily loaded massive handbag – seemingly equipped with brass knuckles or bricks - slides off the shoulder, down the arm, and comes to rest firmly and squarely on an unsuspecting nose. You can be certain the resulting YELP is not one of pleasure.

And women's liberation has only made this brutality more pre-valent. Now that more ladies are working, whatever is in those damned bags weighs one helluva lot more than their prior con-tents. While a ton of feathers may weigh as much as a ton of bricks, I can personally attest that a handbag full of legal briefs weighs a damned site more than one with diapers or shopping coupons.

And with men's liberation, you may also have noticed that a sign of a so-called liberated man is one carrying those cursed boy bags as well. In the old days, at least the men would set their briefcases on the ground or transfer them to the other hand before assaulting us. Not now. Nope. These liberated brothers bend down to pound our heads and, zoom, here comes another shoulder bag!

Listen. Whatever the meritorious benefits are for you bipeds, equal opportunity has meant double physical jeopardy for us. And we don't enjoy the Constitutional protection forbidding double jeopardy. More privileges for you, more physical abuse for us.

Not how we would expect you to treat your 'best friends'.

Maybe we should chew on it for a while……..

Street Scenes

Empty sidewalks are neither interesting nor fun for me.

Happily, the sidewalks as well as the streets of New York are always bustling. And I'm all for it.

And the interesting thing is that my experience seems so totally different than yours. From what I hear, most people find Yorkers - the local argot for Manhattanites, absolutely not to be confused with Yorkies - aloof, cold, rude and unfriendly in the extreme. And I understand that. Even from down here, I see what goes on up there.

When you're walking down the street, you avoid any form of recognition of other people, staring straight ahead to avoid even mere eye contact. In all my years working, er, walking the pavement, I've yet to see a stranger stop to talk with another. Panhandle, yes. But really talk, actually converse? Never. A rare friend, perhaps; but even that is rushed, even terse.

My experience is totally different. I can't tell you how often I am stopped by complete strangers, most of whom – in addition to assaulting me as I have just described - want to pass a bit of time in what they consider conversation.

To be honest, Yorkers' conversational skills are, shall we say, limited and oddly startlingly personal: "What's your name?" "What type of dog are you?" "How old are you?"

Know what I'm thinking to myself while this blather is delaying my progress? "None of your friggin' business!" "Wag tail; floppy ears; walk on four legs. What kind of dog can I be?!? What kind of human are YOU??" "Old enough to know better than to play this silly game. Go assault someone your own size!!"

These encounters make even cats seem smart and interesting. But more about cats shortly.

Worse, encounters like these are not in any way solicited. I don't go up to people I don't know, stand in their path, bob back and forth continuing to block their way if they try to move around me, insisting upon some form of social interaction.

Let's face it, even if I wanted to, I'm quite short and by your standards skinny. In other words, my 14 pounds are no match for a determined Yorker intent on catching the 5:15 out of Grand Central. No way. No, these little gatherings are always initiated by you.

As much as these brief encounters make the place friendlier, after a while they can get to be a real bore.

Besides, I have my own reasons for being out there. There are certain personal matters to attend to. And, while the streets are nothing more than a means of getting from one place to another for you, they happen to be my bathroom, recreation, exercise and entertainment as well.

That means I want to spend my time sniffing around, checking out what and who have been there ahead of me, and I want to be on the move. So to be forced to stand still and appear interested in some perfectly inane comment from someone I've never seen before and never will again is not my idea of a fun time.

Now, if on the other hand you would offer me a luscious smelling treat………..

The only competition that Pepper seems to have for similar attention of passing strangers are baby carriages. They too have the ability to stop even bustling Yorkers in their tracks, though not nearly as often…..something in which I confess to taking some quiet pride.

Making the Beast, 'er Best of It

Happily, despite or perhaps because of my discomfort with these encounters, TOM has found ways to handle them in a way that gives us both our own private pleasure.

For example, when the "What's your name?" question is asked, after allowing me a period to answer he'll finally speak up with names such as Father Flanagan, Attila the Hun, Kirby the Third, El Greco, Donald Parton, Two-Ton Tony, Flipper, Spumonte, Elsinore. During a particularly fraught period in New York, Son of Sam was good for a chuckle or two.

To the "What kind of dog are you", it doesn't seem to matter how TOM answers this question, the reaction is always the same. At first, TOM would give the straight answer, "Miniature Schnauzer". To which the reaction would be either, "Oh yes, my neighbor used to have one" or "I've heard of those." "Those!" Like I am some sort of freak!

Bored with the endless real or pretend familiarity and repetition, TOM started having some fun. Now he'll answer with whatever nonsense pops into his head at the time. Recent examples include, "He's a Canadian anteater." "African mountain dog."

"South American husky." "Southwestern snow-dog." "Scottish eland." "Georgian hunter".

None of these or any of the other imaginary breeds has made one bit of difference in the replies. "Oh, yes, my neighbor used to have one." Or, "I've heard of those." Really????? That snort you hear from down here? My editorial comment.

Another recurring question is, "How does he like living in the City?" You gotta' admit, this one is right up there with, "Have you stopped beating your wife?" Why don't you try to figure out an answer that makes any kind of sense. Tom's repertoire has included, "I have no friggin' clue. Ask him." Or, "I don't know, we're just visiting from Montana." "He hates it; but I enjoy being cruel to animals." "He didn't like it at first, but his shrink thinks he is beginning to like it." Now, there's a New York answer if ever there was one!

Then there's , "Can I pet him?" Just how fierce do you imagine a 14 pound miniature Schnauzer appears? And how much fun do you think it is for me to have my head pounded, ears pulled or neck scratched by complete strangers?

What's more, you have to understand what this looks like from my perspective. I'm what you would call short: my head is closer to your ankle than your knee. I weigh c. 14 pounds versus even the skinniest of you at 100+ pounds, though to be honest too many of you seem to spend way too much time at your food bowls. True I can run faster, but remember I am tethered to TOM; my radius of safety is perilously circumscribed. To say strangers of your size are threatening is a mild understatement.

TOM knows well my feelings about this, having witnessed any number of near-death experiences - not for me but for my assailant. I may be small, but I can be fierce!

Worse, the question is too frequently simultaneously accompanied by a hand reaching perilously close to my head.

TOM will back me away and try to keep me out of harm's way. He'll try to be polite by explaining, "Only if you want to lose some fingers." Or, "Only if you've had your rabies shot."

Childish Exception

But we do make exceptions when it comes to small children. I guess it is part of our campaign to instill a love of dogs in the newer generation, although we've never discussed it. We always give the little ones a chance to get to know me, "up close and personal" as it were.

However, this involves a certain level of risk, since you can never be certain where their well-intentioned but uncoordinated limbs and fingers will land. Mommy or Daddy will say to their precious bundle of joy "Now pat the nice doggy gently on the head." And the next thing I know, I have five sticky fingers in an ear or eye, sometimes both. Simultaneously.

Simple cooers are okay, though. Just fine in fact. In all the world, there's no more endearing sound than the gurgle of a happy baby. Besides, sometimes, just enough to make the risks worthwhile, I'll get lucky and enjoy, take great delight in a truly delicious lick of ice cream or candy. Whisker-licking heaven!

Screamers on the other hand are another matter altogether. Between the high-pitched squealing and the mindless flailing of what seems like countless limbs, my canine ministry is cut short and I'm outta' there.

And something else about you so-called adults. When accompanied by a wee bairn, you seem to think it necessary to make silly noises when you pass me on the street. While universally inane, what's interesting about this little quirk is that there is a real gender difference in the noises you make.

Men bark. Women coo.

Let me ask you men something. How dumb do you think I am? When you bark at me, do you expect me to stop, say to myself, "Ah hah, another dog. I think I'll go take a sniff." Do you really want me to start sniffing your tail? Or, now that I think of it, are you trying to tell me you want to sniff my tail? Either way, that's a little too strange, even for Yorkers, certainly for me.

As for you women, either way coos don't work for me. You know what coo's sound like to me? Pigeons. Of which there are aplenty in these parts. Even if your legs do look better than theirs, and certainly are better shod, best stick to your own breed.

My advice to you?

Do all of us a favor.

Keep on shovin'!

Almost invariably when parting from one of these encounters with a baby carriage, the accompanying adult – looking adoringly down at the child - will say something like, "Isn't he/she the cutest thing ever!?" to which I respond, "Why, thank you very much."

A Higher Perspective

It's true. Walking New York's streets with Pepper is a constant adventure. New York, and Manhattan in particular, has the reputation, mostly well deserved, of being cold and impersonal. And that's been my experience too, by and large. But having a dog makes a huge difference.

For reasons I've never understood, while strangers never dream of approaching each other, they don't think twice about stopping to talk to, with, or about dogs.

Out by myself, not once have I been stopped or approached by anyone other than a panhandler. Thankfully. It'd almost certainly scare the hell out of me if I were.

But let me have Pepper along, and we are always being stopped with the comments always, always directed to or about him. Even when the other person is not accompanied by another dog.

But when two dog walkers meet, most often a strange relationship develops, one characteristic of and perhaps unique to New York. The most intimate details are shared about the dogs, but typically not even names are exchanged between the people.

I can't tell you how many dogs I have met where the dogs'

names are promptly exchanged along with other seemingly relevant data like breed, gender and age and then over time, medical histories, behavioral quirks and recent adventures.... exactly the sort of updates friends would have with each other except we humans are speaking on behalf of our respective dogs...with nary a word about ourselves.

As an example, Pepper has mentioned my occasional extended business trips. On returning, when back out on the street with Pepper and bumping into our dog walking friends, their comments are always, "We've not seen Pepper for a while and wondered if he was OK."

I'm not pointing fingers. I've done exactly the same thing myself.

This "street-smart safety" of studied anonymity seems inbred in native Yorkers, and is quickly adopted by those like me who have migrated into The City.

But as with any rule, there is always an exception.

Amid the dozens of dogs I've met and gotten to know while knowing nothing about who's at the other end of the leash, there is one glorious exception: Helen and her pet companion, a white toy poodle, Melina.

Melina and Pepper have a 'thing' for each other, both delighted as can be when they meet. After their joyful yelping and romping in circles at the end of their leashes, Pepper will of course move around for a good sniff at the back end. To which Melina's response - even though she's as female as they come - is to lift her rear leg. Which is why Helen refers to Melina as "The Hooker of Second Avenue."

Now Pepper - as you may have guessed – is a wee bit spoiled. Melina, on the other hand, may have invented the term. After all, how many dogs do you know with custom-made mink jackets?

The joy the two dogs take in each other is heartwarming, indeed; so I'd be favorably disposed to Helen in any event. But what endears me to this utterly charming lady is that she is well into her 70's, still presides - or should I say, lords - over a bustling flower shop on Madison Avenue with a dozen frantically busy staff, and is as feisty and full of life as if she were half her age. And the crowning glory? A mouth like a very, very angry long-shoreman.

Bumping into Helen and Melina at the end of a work day, I might be greeted with: "Busiest fucking day of the week. Don't know how we ever got all those goddamned orders delivered. Wish to hell those bastards would give us more than a few hours' notice next time. Selfish, egotistical sons-of-bitches. Who the hell do they think we are, their fuckin' slaves? Oh, I'm fine, dear, and so is Melina; and how are you and dear little Pepper?"

You gotta love a lady like that; and believe me, I do.

The Most Dangerous Day of the Year

Being a Schnauzer - German to the core - you wouldn't think I would harbor ill-will toward celebrations by fellow Europeans also now resident in these United States marking their national holidays. As you well know, I'm all for marking anything and everything.

Part of what makes New York special is this mixture of breeds from all over the world. On any given weekend once the weather even hints of spring, you can depend upon a parade up or down Fifth Avenue, complete with marching politicians wagging their tails and picnicking immigrants who leave behind a delightful smorgasbord of snacks on the Avenue and in Central Park for those of us with some civic pride to clean up afterwards. Being free to frolic in the Park on a Sunday afternoon following the Parade du Jour is nearly as heavenly as Second Avenue in August during a garbage strike: endless opportunities to satiate the senses! I am an Equal Opportunity Glutton: all marchers are welcome to leave their particular residue.

There is, however, one notable exception to my ecumenical policy, reflecting an accident of geography. You see, where I live in New York just off Second Avenue in the 40's, is an area dense with Irish pubs. This means that on St. Patrick's Day, the contents of these normally self-contained establishments spill out onto the sidewalks. Literally hanging onto parking meters, leaning against buildings and draped over any pedestrians not quick enough to get out of the way will be a gaggle of Irishmen and even more wannabes, several sheets to the wind and screaming for more canvas.

The real Irish add to the festivities by dressing in their native garb, which means a great many kilts, knees, too many ill-tuned and worse played bagpipes screeching like the stuck critters from which the bags were made, all accompanied by chorus after chorus of blubbering "Oh Danny Boy" punctuated by bottles breaking on the pavement.

This whole unruly hoard is Erin Go Braugh-ing to beat all hell.

The visual and audible assaults are like no other, even for New York.

Fun is fun, I grant you. But you try navigating through a forest of densely packed redwoods with their massive trunks and bare knees weaving and bobbing all over the place making ear-splitting sounds either vocally or instrumentally – sometimes both at the same time - especially if you're my size.

Imagine yourself wandering the narrow streets of Lower Manhattan, huge buildings all around you each emitting its unique cacophony concurrently.

Makes being drawn and quartered seem more than kind, right?!

And then there is the safety risk of the sidewalks. When's the last time you tried walking bare-foot through dozens of broken beer bottles and whiskey glasses, accompanied by occasional pools of disgorged beer and bangers?!?

Now I know why they're called Irish Setters. Living with the Irish, setting is by far the only sane thing to do.

Don't think for a minute that Pepper has exaggerated a thing. It's all true. And the residual stench, and small shards of glass, last for days. The only silver lining in this otherwise bleak cloud is that the stretch of Irish pubs on Second Avenue only runs north of where we live and, here's the best part, on every block, there is only one. That means that it's still possible to walk north by crisscrossing from one side of the Avenue to the other as needed.

This is important as certain goods are only available at stores to the north.

The best solution is for me to be abroad for St. Patrick's Day as there are no Irish Pubs near Bonnie's apartment.

TOM, Me and the Ladies

As a bachelor, TOM is not always to be trusted around unaccompanied women. While most of the time he's on his good behavior, let an especially attractive woman see us and say, "Oh, how cute." And he'll say, "Him or me?"

Or she'll make those sexy kissing sounds. "Are they for him or for me?" Honestly! I can't tug him away fast enough.

Look, I don't interfere in Pepper's sidewalk adventures with those he finds of interest. It's annoying that he doesn't allow me the same latitude.

I'll tell you what the difference is. I'm neutered and he's not. If he gets himself neutered, I'll happily let him flirt as much as he wants.

Tethered to TOM

All week, whenever outside I'm tethered to TOM, which means that I pretty much have to go where he wants to go and at his pace. If I want to head off on my own, to follow a scent or check out a tree, I have to put my nose to the pavement and tug for all I'm worth.

You'd be surprised how much of a pull a 14 pound Schnauzer can exert when he puts his mind to it. If he was an 80 pound lab, I would have been drawn and quartered long ago.

Or we may be marching along - TOM's typical gait is a Sgt. Major's pace - when a garbage bag or tree well catches my interest. I'll pause while TOM continues. To satisfy my curiosity, I have to dig in, which is not easy to do on concrete, thereby producing an uncomfortable yank on my neck - and his arm.

Dripped dry, I weigh in at 14 pounds; TOM at 155. For me to win any of these directional battles takes both strength and stubbornness on my part, two Teutonic traits we both seem to share in abundance. My only advantages are I have four contact points to pull with against his two, my lower center of gravity, and in dire circumstances sharper teeth with which his butt is already quite familiar. Fortunately, his butt and brain are connected.

The downside to this nightly tug-of-war is that progress from point A to point B can be tediously slow. I may have envisioned a brisk walk enjoying the cool night air, while the other end of the leash almost always has something else in mind or more accurately up his nose.

I confess to occasional impatience. I mean, a 5 or 10 second sniff should be enough, right? But there are times when I start moving and pulling, even yanking on Pepper's leash.

Meeting resistance and feeling particularly impatient, I've been known to look down angrily only to face his withering glare telling me, "Heh, I'm just being a dog, dumbass. Get a grip!"

For five long tedious days, whenever not in the apartment, my freedom is circumscribed by a six foot strip of nylon.

 Don't get me wrong: you know how much I love, love, LOVE the streets of New York and all the joys and delights they offer.

But these delights do have a string attached, actually something far stronger: a leash. Now, you have to understand this is one of your inventions which are totally foreign and even contrary to our natural state. Little wonder that it takes us some time, often accompanied by some pain, to learn to live with it. Eventually at some point most of us come to accept it as a small price to pay for sharing our lives with you. But don't misunderstand: accepting it is not the same as liking it.

Think I'm being unreasonable?

Try it sometime and see how much you like it.

Pepper, as he annoyingly does with some frequency, has a point: dogs are not biologically equipped or prepared not to be free, despite hundreds of years of so-called domestication. Putting dogs on leashes is messing around with Mother Nature: it may be necessary or at the least prudent, but it is unnatural for our pet companions.

To illustrate the point about efforts to change or mess around with biological imperatives, I want to share a long-ago experience while attending, out of curiosity along with other school friends, a tent-revival meeting back in W.VA. where I grew up.

The preacher was addressing the packed tent and overflow crowd outside, talking about various sins, one of which even in the early 1950's was smoking. To drive his point home he bellowed in his best Hillbilly twang, "If God had wanted you to smoke, He would have put a smokestack on your head!!!"

Note: We don't come equipped with leashes.

S'now Fun

When it snows in New York, we dogs are in for a very difficult and painful time. Let one snowflake fall and the City's Sanitation Department panics, one manifestation of which is it rolls out behemoth machines that move up and down the main avenues, snow plows in front and, take special note here, salt-spreaders in the rear spewing sodium chloride from curb to curb and sometimes beyond.

Taking their cue from Your Government In Action, every landlord and maintenance man rushes to mimic the effort on their entries and sidewalks. They may or may not shovel or sweep the snow or ice aside but you can be certain that every square inch of concrete will be turned into one endless salt flat.

Any snowfall from a light dusting to a major Nor'easter produces the same reaction and consequence. The streets and sidewalks of Manhattan turn into the great salt lakes out West. The entire island is one humongous salt-lick.

So far that makes sense to you, right? Keeps you from falling and scratching your new shoes or tearing your hose or ripping your coat or spraining or breaking your wrist or whatever?

Neither snow nor rain nor heat nor gloom of night stays true Yorkers from the swift completion of their appointed rounds, right?

So what's the problem you ask? With a solid surface of salt replacing soft snow or even hard ice, you've got needed traction. Know what we've got? We've got pain! I'm talking searing, stinging hurt here.

You know the phrase, "Salt in an open wound?" Ever have it happen to you? Remember what it feels like? It hurts like hell, that's what it feels like.

Now, imagine walking down New York's sidewalks - now a solid bed of salt - in your bare feet. Further imagine what your feet are gonna feel like, once the salt starts working its way into any small cracks in your skin.

Beginning to get the picture?

Well, imagine this with all four feet. It's bloody awful and cruel, that's what it is.

The natural instinct is to lift all four paws off the pavement, just as you would instinctively pull your hands if both were touching a too-hot surface. Simple animal instinct. Mother Nature's way of protecting us from harm.

While Mother Nature's instilled instinct works well for you, not so much for us. The best we can do is lift one stinging paw at a time and when it's tolerable lower it and lift another. The sad, painful dance-like cycle of lifting and lowering of searing paws may strike some of you as a source of mirth. SHAME ON YOU!!!!

You should know that laughing at another's discomfort is quite inhumane.

Hint to Sanitation Departments, Landlords, Building Superintendents, and Owners everywhere: stick with sand and gravel or risk a canine revolt that will not end well for you!

The Scoop on the Scooper

It was during my early youth that the good burghers of New York - definitely not my type of burgers - enacted what came to be known far and wide as The Pooper Scooper Law.

This civic minded effort at reining in and preventing the wanton destruction of one of the world's preeminent cities has annoyed me to no end, if you catch my drift. For those of you unfamiliar with this civic chicanery, the self-same burghers included a fine of at least $50 on anyone caught not picking up after we've done what some of you ever so delicately call, "Number Two." In other words, you get crapped on if you don't pick up ours.

If you get caught, that is. And that's where I take exception. To make myself perfectly clear, I applaud – or would if I could –the law itself. As I have mentioned, I can't cover up my poop so having someone pick it up on my behalf is a sound, sensible - if sniff-defying - civic and environmentally sensitive requirement.

Besides, it's had some unintended and quite amusing consequences. Let me tell you about those first before explaining the less entertaining reasons for my reservations about the new Law.

By now, no doubt there are half-a-dozen doctoral theses crowding university library shelves based on the sociological, psychological, perhaps even economic analyses of pooper scoopers. This being New York, there is, after all, a fascinating spectrum.

There are the little old ladies with their newly manufactured and outrageously overpriced plastic instruments, looking very much like the proverbial ten-foot pole, at the end of which is an urban equivalent of a bear trap, over which is draped a plastic bag.

Once the offending evidence is presented, it can be enwrapped in the plastic bag and the package deposited in the nearest trash bin totally untouched by human hands which have come no closer than several feet to the entire operation. Now there's an inspired application of engineering to sanitation deserving of admiration if not its inflated price tag.

Then there are the practical, even cheap, types, of which TOM I'm proud to say is one. They simply carry a supply of little plastic sandwich bags. Given the need, they put their hands into a bag, pick up the matter, pull the bag off their hand and thus over the subject, thereby wrapping it as neatly as a sandwich and then deposit it in the next available trash bin. Simple, direct, gets the job done with a minimum of fuss.

Talk about unintended consequences. I no longer have to add identification tags to any of my clothes. They're the ones with the little plastic bags in all the pockets. I now know what my mother had to go through to wash my clothes: a thorough search of every pocket to remove whatever rested therein. My search needs to be just as thorough but focused exclusively on finding small plastic bags. I actually found one once in the outside vest pocket of a sport coat. Don't ask.

Of course, there is the question of an appropriate - as in sufficient - size of the needed bag. I'm a little Schnauzer; so a small sandwich bag does just fine. But many dogs are larger, some much more so.

For example one of our neighbors has 5 mini-dachshunds and 1 Russian hound dog. Proper size is important.

Pepper's best friend is a huge white Samoyed, Ralph, who lives with his human companion, Ben, in our apartment building. More about both later. But for now, the four of us typically go out together for a mid-evening walk. Ben's graphically descriptive term for Big Ralph's deposit is a "Plopper" for which he is suitably equipped with a supply of grocery store plastic bags.

Then there is the newspaper brigade. No long-handled instruments or plastic bags for this crowd, no siree. Nope, these folks really get down and dirty, the state of newsprint being what it is.

There are two categories. Most seem content to let us do our thing, after which they do theirs, picking up ours with a wad of today's Daily News or The Post. Where we live in Manhattan no one would ever think of using The Times or Wall Street Journal for such purposes.

But my favorites are those who intervene earlier in the process. What happens is this. We'll signal our intentions by stopping and hunching down. The name of the game now becomes, "Who Gets There First?" The human half's role in this comedy is trying to place the newspaper in exactly the right location at precisely the right moment to catch what the whole exercise is all about. This takes a remarkable degree of hand-eye coordination as well as a reasonably cooperative, that is unmoving, partner. Off just a bit on either timing or location, and the whole process becomes considerably messier.

Sometimes you'll see one of us decide to have a little fun and then it can get really comical. We'll pause and hunch over. The other actor quickly bends over and strategically places some newspaper. We'll then straighten up and move along, leaving nothing behind, only to circle, pause and hunch over again a few paces later. The paper again hits the ground but nothing else. And so on down the street until either we've had enough fun or nature takes over. Puts bobbing for apples to shame!

And it's also how we go about paper-training you. Ah, sweet revenge.

Comic and bowel relief aside, what makes me mad about the Pooper-Scooper Law is its uneven and inconsistent enforcement.

It's bad enough that half the time it's a law officer on horseback who's the enforcer. Talk about the pot calling the kettle black! I mean the sheer lunacy of a mounted cop ticketing some poor poodle for its meager deposit while at same time the horse's is putting another dent into the street.

Look. In the broad scheme of things, with all the illegal activity going on at any given moment on any given day anywhere and everywhere in the five boroughs of New York, should one minute of anyone's time be spent enforcing this particular law?

I know it is said of money that if you watch the pennies, the dollars will take care of themselves. But when it comes to crime, life, health, and safety in New York, I wonder if perhaps the situation isn't a wee bit different.

Honestly, don't you have the feeling deep down that when it comes to priorities, that maybe, just maybe, there might be a few other infractions that ought to command the attention of the authorities?

That's one thing I don't like about New York: the distorted priorities: grabbing the wrong end of the Pooper-Scooper stick, if you ask me.

Once a City Dog...

Don't for a minute get the idea from what Pepper has just said that he would prefer to do his business any place other than on a Manhattan sidewalk. Why, when he was first taken outside and given the chance to explore the City, all he experienced was concrete.

Once sufficiently older and was first taken to Central Park, he wouldn't even get off the pavement! He'd walk in that unsteady gait of all puppies right up to the edge of the walkway, drop his head and ever so slowly poke his nose towards the unfamiliar expanse of soft, green stuff. He'd give it a good sniff and then bolt back to the safety of the middle of the concrete or blacktop. I'd encourage him from the rear or pull him from the front. He'd have none of it. Whatever that green stuff was, he wasn't having any part of it, thank you very much.

Even after he got over his initial resistance to grass and got to quite enjoy romping freely in the Park, frolicking over the lawns, into the bushes, around the trees, through the shrubs, absolutely free and uncaring in his explorations, comes time for business and he'll divert his course, find a suitable walkway, hunch over and proceed. Hundreds of acres of grass and dirt and he insists on a paved surface!

And not just in Central Park. Anywhere he goes. Beaches in Georgia or Cape Cod? Use any of that sandy stuff? Nope, right to and on the driveway. The beach on Long Island? Ditto. Upstate New York? In the woods? Nope, right on the highway.

You've heard of animals that head for the sandbox? Not this fella! He wants pavement.

This has gone on for years, so that when we headed to New Hampshire for a summer vacation at a lakeside cottage down a gravel road more than a mile off the paved highway, I couldn't help but wonder. While I had no idea what Pepper was going to do, I knew for certain that on my vacation I wasn't about to hike a mile several times a day, including at 6 a.m. just so he could feel a familiar firmness underfoot. Even for him I have limits.

Well, I want you to know the little devil had his way, nearly. There we were, smack in the middle of a beautiful, rustic setting, with a magnificent lake 20 yards dead ahead, no neighbors within fifty yards, and that gravel road 40 yards up a dirt driveway from the cottage. I mean, plenty of grass, lots of bushes and trees, all resting nicely on good, solid hard clay and rocky New Hampshire soil. Where did Pepper insist on going in order to go? Yup, out to that gravel road!

He'd water everything upright within a 30 yard radius. But when it came time for the other, right out to the gravel.

In fairness to him and to be honest with you, his behavior was not the only strange one on display. Not a New York City Copper within hundreds of miles, out in the country where dogs and leashes aren't even on speaking terms, and there I was with plastic bags at the ready, still playing City Slicker!

Tickling Traits

Every dog has his or her own habits and cute little quirks, or ones that to you - objective as you are - think are cute. I'm not talking about what we teach them to do. I'm talking about traits, habits or patterns of behavior they develop all by themselves. No human intervention. Completely self-taught.

Some are not in the cute category at all. Like chewing shoes. Ripping upholstery. Unrolling toilet paper - although this one seems to me a borderline case. Emptying wastebaskets. Stealing food from the counter, or the garbage. Hiding your fill-in-the-

blank - the best example of which I ever heard was diaphragm. Aspects of their personalities and behavior that you would just as soon do without.

But happily our canine friends just as often develop far more endearing traits. Walking down the street holding its own leash. Rolling over to have its tummy rubbed when you get home. Climbing up and looking out the window when you're due home. Riding on the ledge over the back seat in the car. Sitting by the door when it needs to be outside for reasons of personal hygiene. Fetching the paper and not using it for anything else. Sleeping at the foot of the bed under the covers, somehow managing not to suffocate but providing a built-in foot warmer. Lying quietly at your feet with its head on your toes. Licking you on your nose to let you know it's time to go out first thing in the morning.

You know, little behavioral quirks that spring from nowhere and help define what makes your pup special.

Pepper naturally has his share, although I am quite fortunate in that he has absolutely none that I wished he didn't have. In all the years we've been together, he hasn't destroyed a single item.

The closest he comes to being truly annoying is when he grows either impatient or overly-excited with our preparing to go certain places. I've already told you about how excited he gets when he's figured out he's going to Bonnie's, jumping up and down, nipping my butt.

The only other destination that triggers the same exuberance complete with butt-bites is when I've asked him if he wants to go to the Park. First he'll jump onto the chair closest to the front door, stand up with his front paws on the back of the chair, raise his head, purse his lips and howl. Then he races to the front door from which his leash is hanging, starts to jump up and down and almost dares me to put it around his neck. Once the door is opened ever so slightly, he forces it open enough to bolt to the elevator pulling me after him. Then, heaven help us - and especially my tush - if the elevator doesn't arrive quickly enough.

But once we're on the street and trying to hail a cab, he calms down, lays quietly on my lap during the ride, walks purposely without tugging until we're inside the Park at which time he waits patiently for me to remove the leash then off he gleefully runs.

I follow, discretely rubbing my butt.

But that's about it. Otherwise, I really can't think of anything he does, or doesn't do, that I wish were different.

On the other hand, it will come as no surprise to you if I report that there is a goodly amount of his natural behavior that I find charming and endearing and cute. Three in particular stand out, only one of which can on occasion prove nettlesome.

The one that is mostly cute but infrequently not is Pepper hates closed doors. This is oddly selective and only manifests itself when he's confronted by one that shuts him out from a place he thinks he has every right and a keen interest in being inside. Most doors don't trigger his get-in-at-all-costs response. Closet doors don't seem to matter even if I'm hiding inside. Nor the door into the apartment. Bathroom doors when I am inside are a tossup: sometimes he wants in and sometimes not. But a closed bedroom door? That's guaranteed to get him going, and wanting in...badly.

He's utterly unselfconscious about this. It makes absolutely no difference who is inside. He wants in. He is abetted in his endeavors since it's an older pre-war (Spanish, I believe) New York apartment meaning that the door no longer quite closes nor does the latch quite latch. In short, he gets in and hops on the bed. Then he proceeds to make a thorough check of everything ....and everyone.

Before Bonnie and I separated, this trait was more cute than not. But after I was single again, well, not so much. On some occasions it has led to my getting an ultimatum, phrased in varying degrees of delicacy or directness but always boiling down to, "It's him or me." Sometimes that has presented the need for extreme delicacy and diplomacy while on other times, I've secretly rejoiced.

And just in case you are wondering, there is absolutely no truth whatsoever to the rumor that I have trained him to do this. It is entirely his own creation. On the other hand, I could have had that latch fixed.....

A particularly endearing trait is when I arrive home unexpectedly and the startled look of surprise on his face when I walk through the apartment door and surprise him.

He'd have been sound asleep on the sofa, and at the sound of the key in the lock he would come partway awake and kind of sleepily glance at the door to see which apartment worker was coming in to fix a drip. Or so the guys in the apartment would report. They'd enter, Pepper would confirm the identity from his prone position, never bothering to bestir himself for a closer look; and put his head back down and return to sleep. Some watch dog!

But when, through his half-closed eyes, he saw me rather than someone who could safely be ignored, the most startled look comes over his face. His ears pick right up; his eyes grow wide; his head jerks up to full extension; and his whole demeanor cries out, "Hey, whatthehell? Is that you? What are you doing here at this hour?" followed by a bolt to the door and an especially joyful greeting.

Yet another one: Pepper seems to think that he and only he is responsible for disrobing anything that comes into the house wrapped. Bring home the groceries, and he will tear open the paper bags - this was back in the days before those convenient if environmentally unfriendly plastic carrying bags came into fashion. Surprisingly he shows little or no interest in what's inside, even if it is boxed or wrapped; those are just another layer to be dealt with. SOS pads or crackers – couldn't care less. And it's not just food. Bring home a package from the stationery store, the haberdasher, even the hardware store. Same thing. Rips the bejesus out of it.

Family birthdays and Christmas are great fun. Once each item is hand-delivered to the intended destination, the giftee has willing and eager assistance, more accurately persistence in getting to the goods.

This obsession with the packaging rather than the contents surprisingly extends to his own. No matter how much thought and effort go into picking out something different or a new kind of chew or a different toy, Pepper is happiest simply ripping open the package, every package. He's far more selective in deciding which contents will or will not be of further interest.

And he is thorough. If the shredded wrapping hasn't been removed, he'll make return trips to see if anything may have escaped his attention. He'll vigorously shake a balled-up wad of paper or gift wrapping just to be sure.

Christmas, of course, is Nirvana. The custom of the house he came into was many little gifts exchanged between Bonnie and me and my Dad rather than one or two big ones. Naturally we applied the same rule to Pepper. Little did we know the boon this would prove to be. Ever see a dog so delighted with an abundance of riches that he clearly can't make up his mind where to turn next, eagerly looking for the next target of opportunity? The living room floor soon looked like several paper shredders had hemorrhaged simultaneously. What's more, this trait did not carry over to the outside.

As he accompanies me on many trips outside which result in one or more paper bags to tote home, his fascination with those packages manifests itself very differently. Rather than shredding the bags, anything he can manage to carry in his mouth he eagerly joins in the toting. No kidding. If you put, say, an apple into a little paper bag and reach down, Pepper will take it ever so gently at the top of the bag and then carry it back to the apartment.

It doesn't make any difference what is inside: an apple, some bread, a roll of toilet paper, something from the hardware store, it doesn't have to be edible or even have an appealing scent. All it has to be is wrapped in a paper bag, not too heavy or oversized, just manageable. But he always eagerly volunteers and is willing to try anything no matter the size or weight. So I'll always let him try.

Too large or bulky and while he'll try valiantly, if the ballast isn't right or if he stumbles behind it while making the effort, he'll drop it and carry on, without looking back.

But once he's got a good grip and feels at ease, he is determined. Up come the head, ears and tail, and he literally prances down the street with a determined, purposeful stride. Officious might not be too strong.

That little dog has his mind made up, is proud of what he is doing, and nothing is going to get in the way of completing his task. Everything about him says, "Out of my way, Buster; I'm on a mission." The Postal Service should take lessons from this guy.

Of course once he gets home, he figures that since he's done all the work, the fruits of his labors are in his teeth. Not that he wants to eat whatever's inside; he simply wants to open the damned thing.

Separating him from his package is never easy, and it almost always takes a little treat to distract his attention and to get his jaws to open. In other words, he has trained me very well.

As much as I always enjoy watching these little performances from above and to the rear, what makes them so wonderfully special is watching the reactions of people coming the other way on the crowded streets of Manhattan, striding that determined Yorker march.

There are those who insist on showing just how cool, how blasé they really are by pretending not to notice while I see their beady little eyes look down at him. The head tilts up taking with it the nose, but those beady little eyes still stay fixed on Pepper.

At the other end of the spectrum are those, happily more in number, who stop dead in their tracks, permitting themselves to be temporarily diverted from their tasks, who pause to admire Pepper's behavior, almost always then looking up at me as I pass by, giving me an appreciative look and possibly even a smile.

But my favorites are those who see Pepper coming and whose paces slow a bit, who look first down at Pepper then up at me then back to Pepper, and whose faces break out into the most endearing, unrestrained grins. Possibly even a mirthful chuckle. I mean, the sheer glee they get from it!

For all I know, some of these folks are wife-beaters or child abusers or serial killers. Most seem pretty stressed out, as almost everyone on Manhattan's streets always looks. Maybe they have just been fired or divorced or have come within one digit of winning the lottery. But no matter how pressured or hectic or worrisome their lives may be and probably are, they see Pepper and his bag and permit themselves to be distracted if only for a brief moment and to find a bit of joy.

I can't tell you how much pleasure I take in theirs. For no matter how stressed I am and preoccupied with my own hassles, seeing the delight on their faces always brings a stupid grin to my own. In taking such joy from Pepper, they are giving at least as much to me.

All from one little grey dog on the busy streets of New York!

<u>City Adventures</u>

Dining Out

You wouldn't think that I would get the chance to go to many restaurants, would you? This is the United States, after all. A civilized country. Not a primitive place like France, where we are not only permitted but welcomed even in the finest five-star establishments. No, the good ol' USofA is far too refined.

Au contraire.

When I was younger, about once every two months or so I would get the chance to eat out in a quite nice Manhattan restaurant. Here's how.

At the time my best friend was a magnificent white Samoyed named Ralph who lived in the same apartment building. When I got to know him, Ralph was already a senior citizen, well along in years and increasingly plagued by arthritis. Always eager of heart, Ralph's movements were somewhat hindered by a combination of age and infirmity. Willing but labored, I'd guess you'd say.

Sadly, Ralph's human companion, Ben, was himself afflicted with a degenerative eye disease and was even then legally blind. "Uncle Ben" was an enormously warm and gentle fellow, great company and, like TOM a real dog lover.

As it happened, TOM and Uncle Ben hit it off as well, so the four of us used to spend a lot of time together.

Ralph, Uncle Ben and his wife Wendy occupied one of two penthouses of our building, complete with a huge terrace. TOM and I would be invited up to laze away hot summer evenings dining on the terrace, or in the afternoon to work the Times Sunday puzzle.

TOM would read the clues to Uncle Ben, who would figure the puzzle out in his head. TOM served as scribe writing the answer down in ink as Uncle Ben never made a mistake.

We'd go for our nightly walks together, checking out the neighborhood. On weekends, we'd go hiking in the country, usually prowling around one of the Rockefeller Estates or some other equally splendid Hudson River property. While TOM would serve as Uncle Ben's eyes, I would romp around and shepherd Ralph.

Uncle Ben who began work in the rag trade eventually with a partner opened one of the first single bars in New York City. Over time and with much success the one grew into a chain of high-end eating and drinking establishments on the upper East Side. Those food emporia were the sites of my dining adventures.

Here's what would happen. On a Saturday or Sunday afternoon about 2 or so, the phone would ring and it would be Uncle Ben.

"What are you guys doin'?"

TOM, rather than telling the truth ("Takin' a nap, dummy!") would say, "Nothing, why?"

Uncle Ben: "Let's take the dogs to (and he'd name one of his restaurants)."

TOM, the first time said, "To the restaurant? Isn't that illegal?" Sad but true: TOM is not always the brightest when he first awakens. Me? I would have reacted more positively right away.

Uncle Ben, "Sure, but I own the place; so let's go!"

Shortly thereafter, we'd hit the street, eventually convincing a cabbie to pick the four of us up. I don't know why but it always took more than one try: two guys, two dogs, one the size of a small Shetland pony, what's the problem?!

Eventually we'd arrive at the front door of one of Uncle Ben's places. Over time, we got to visit each one.

Now Uncle Ben didn't own just any ol' watering place. He catered to rich singles and well-off Yuppie couples. In other words, his places were tres chichi 'upscale' and densely popu-lated - at least on early weekend afternoons - with well-to-do East Siders on the make. Which is to say the patrons were pre-dominantly upper-middle class whites taking their brunches and themselves far too seriously.

Imagine what fun Ralph and I would have in those dining rooms!

Picture it. A sleek dining room full of oak, brass and glass; every table occupied with earnest men and beautiful women; Bloody Mary's and wine glasses everywhere; the conversations loud and intense but glowing with proper decorum.

Suddenly some confusion starts by the front door and quickly spreads. A huge white dog slowly lumbers his way around the floor while a little grey one darts from table to table. Disruption ripples around the room.

I don't know if it was because, to them, Ralph probably looked like a polar bear and I must have looked like a tail-less rat on steroids. Some of those people would either sit pretending not to notice the growing mayhem ("At all costs, keep your cool.") while the rest of the room would stand, some screaming, and flail their arms at the invaders. It looked and sounded like a frat party out of control.

While the Yuppies were busy trying to figure out what was afoot, as it were, Uncle Ben and TOM would be convulsing all over themselves, hanging onto each other, their amusement knowing no bounds. Their whoops of glee were clearly discernable above the din rising from the rest of the room, which of course only urged Ralph and me on to greater effort. Within a few short minutes, absolute chaos would be achieved and a complete Yuppie meltdown attained.

Meanwhile, while everything above and around me was going berserk, I was having a field day cleaning up the floor. I can assure you, the number and variety of snacks I consumed on these outings were enormously satisfying. Whatever else you might say about those pretentious folk, they certainly knew how to eat well; and Uncle Ben's kitchens were more than up to the task. Those munchies set Guinness-level delectability records and would remain almost as delicious in my subsequent dreams.

All good things must come to an end, of course. So after total confusion had been reached and Uncle Ben and TOM were barely able to stand, Ralph and I would get summoned back to the front door for our ceremonial exit. Uncle Ben, ever the perfect host, was always the last one out, pausing, I suppose, to offer a word of sympathy and reassurance to his now totally distraught maître d'.

Since Ben was legally blind, you must be wondering, as I used to, just how much of these scenes he was actually able to see. From all appearances, Ben was seeing - and hearing - enough to take total delight from the experience. I think he enjoyed them enormously and relished being able to carry them out, his unique way of finding ways to benefit from his success by sharing it with his beloved Ralph along with Pepper and me. Ben gave new meaning to the concept of being generous to a fault.

Sadly, these entertainments ceased when Ralph's arthritis got so bad that they were no longer possible. But I have never forgotten his deep, barrel-chested "woof" and Pepper's higher "yelp" as one lumbered and the other bolted from table to table causing panic and leaving mayhem in their wake.

Weekend afternoons have never been the same since.

The Day I Went to Work

Since I didn't technically qualify for Take Your Kid to Work days, I only got to go to TOM's office on nights and weekends.

It's not that I wanted it this way, you understand.

To begin with, I wasn't all that fond of how our duties were divided. While he got to go out and play, my assignment was to stay home and guard the homestead.

This arrangement struck me as not only unfair but unwise. I never could quite figure out, if our 'castle' was so important, why I was the one assigned to guard duty. Alone; solo; all fightin' 14 pounds of scary me. As fierce as I might sound to myself, it's hard to believe an experienced burglar - all burglars in New York are experienced, if you can make it here you can make it anywhere - would think he was about to be confronted with a mighty angry German Shepard or pit bull, fangs dripping. How smart was leaving me behind to guard the goods?!??!

Oh how I longed for the day when TOM would pause at the front door and instead of the normal - and superfluous - "Be a good boy today!"- he would instead say, "Come on, let's go!" Alas, over many years, this was one prayer that sadly went unanswered.

It may well be that good things do indeed come to those who lie in, er, and wait. There did finally come a day when I got to go along. This stroke of good fortune, I must quickly add, was not a result of a temporary softening of his heart or of a change in TOM's firm division of duties. Rather a unique combination of circumstances provided the opportunity. Here's what happened.

The Manhattan apartment where TOM and I live is what is called in New York parlance a "pre-war". While this designation is intended to imply architectural character and structural integrity, there is some imprecision as to exactly which war. In our case, judging from the status of such vital signs as plumbing and wiring, I rather suspect ours was the Spanish-American one.

In any event, one January night during what was the coldest of cold snaps to hit the area in years, the building's ancient boiler ceased functioning - a not uncommon occurrence for this mechanical dinosaur. I knew this because at about 2:30 in the morning, TOM and I were awakened by a frightful chill, even though we were at the time snuggled under our electric blanket.

Not only had the boiler gone south taking with it the heat, we were being treated to a flow of terrifically cold air, thanks to our 'charming pre-war' windows whose fit was, shall we say, somewhat less than snug and getting less so as the ancient woodwork shrank with the drop in temperature. A blast of extremely cold air was howling through the house. I mean, the Arctic Express was making very local stops.

TOM did his best to keep us as warm as possible. We must have been quite a sight. He turned on the electric stove, top burners and the oven. He put us both into sweaters; piled more blankets on the bed; turned the electric blanket up to 'high' and held on to me for all we were collectively worth. It even got to the point where we were shivering in synch.

Think of it: syncopated shivers. Has kind of a nice ring, doesn't it? Sounds a whole lot better than it feels, I can tell you!

Even with all of TOM's emergency measures, sleep was out of the question. It's simply not possible for eye-lids to remain closed and stationary when the rest of the body is quivering uncontrollably. So we spent the balance of that endless night trying to maintain some degree of body heat and avoiding any contact with what was outside air now in residence.

Between us we had two noses, four ears, eight limbs and count-less digits to try to keep from frostbite. It made for a long, qui-vering night.

When the sun finally did come up, neither the outside which is to say inside temperature nor the heat did.

And of course, there was a certain routine to which I and various internal organs had grown accustomed that was initiated by the arrival of that particular time of the day.

In short, conditions outside and in notwithstanding, taking me outside could no longer be delayed. Actually, I don't know why TOM even bothered. Even if I had been permitted to attend to matters in the house, he could easily have picked it up, since it would have frozen instantly before it hit the floor.

At least there weren't any more layers to put on before going out. We were already multi-layered and barely mobile. What a sight we must have been, the two of us, waddling down the street.

Since this was far from the first time that the boiler had decided to take a hike, there was no way of knowing if and when it would be restored to life, especially since it was a safe bet that the repair people were likely to be quite busy that day, with many other demands for their attention.

This meant that TOM was faced with the unique problem of what to do with me. Obviously, it would have been too dan-gerous to leave the oven and burners running unattended all day; and even then, it was clear from the night's experience that the outside temperature and wind were more than an even match for the oven. Leaving me in the apartment was out of the question.

Since there were no other arrangements that could be made on such short notice, the only alternative was to take me with him to his office.

Thus after a hurried breakfast and after TOM skipped customary pre-departure rituals - like shaving and, most particularly a shower - off we staggered bundled up in our several sweaters and jackets.

Fortunately his office was only four blocks away, but those were without a doubt the longest four blocks of my life.

Normally upon reaching our destination TOM has to prod and goad me to go inside since I would be much happier if I could stay out and play a little longer. But not that day. Going into his office building seemed to me like a mighty fine idea, thank you very much. I mean, talk about coming in from the cold!

I don't really know how long it took me to thaw out. Most of that day was then and still is a blur. Having been awake all night, cold and miserable as I was, once I got to TOM's warm office most of what I recall is finally being able to stop shivering, slowly warming up, curling up in TOM's lap or on his sofa and getting some long overdue and much needed rest. TOM, on the other hand, poor fellow, had to work, or at least appear to. And of course he had to explain to his colleagues what I was doing there and why he was unshaven and not a little bedraggled.

Imagine what the office wits must have conjured up from their evil hearts and wee minds.

So while I finally got to go along, there is very little I actually remember about that day at TOM's office, except for one quite precious incident.

It occurred the first time TOM took me downstairs to empty my tanks. Under normal circumstances, I would look around for an attractive and appropriate spot along the curb for a tree, fire hydrant, sign post, garbage bin, all the usual places.

Not that frigid morning. No siree. No aimless wandering or careful selectivity that day. As soon as we got outside, I went for and on the first upright item I could find. It so happened to be a pillar adjacent to the front door.

As luck would have it, while I was standing there, leg up and giving it my all, who comes by on his way into the building? Yup, sure enough, TOM's boss!

Talk about embarrassing. Not me; I was relieved. But you can imagine TOM's reaction. Awkward!

Want to know a secret?

I suspect TOM was jealous.

Truth be told, Pepper's not far from the truth, spot on it you might say. By that time, I'd become somewhat skeptical, even disappointed in the new, young and, it seemed to me, overly self-absorbed new president and had begun to think about moving on. While still committed to my work, the organizational environment had become such that what Pepper was doing at that moment seemed to me more appropriate than not.

Canine Yorker

There are those who say that living in New York City is an oxymoron. Well, let me tell you what my life is like, and you can then decide for yourself.

There are instances where being a dog in New York has certain advantages over being a human. For example, since we're not permitted on the subways, we always get to take cabs.

I can pee anytime and anywhere I want or need to, except of course at home.

To shop means selecting from an array of charming boutiques in lieu of the sharp-edged elbows and crowds of Macy's, Saks and Bloomingdale's.

TOM can get me an appointment with a vet on short notice if needed - a mixed blessing - while he typically has to wait weeks to get an appointment with any of his health care providers.

TOM shops for groceries for both of us, and deals with the cleaners and druggists, 'though sometimes I get to tag along.

While he's breathing the cleaners' chemicals, I'm outside relishing the smorgasbord of smells baked into the sidewalks of Manhattan.

And we never have to put up with surly waiters.

On the other hand, there are some disadvantages.

For example, we never get bones to chew on. When's the last time you saw one of us parading down Second Avenue with more calcium in our mouths than the initial equipment? I don't know why we're subjected to this deprivation. Those of us who live in cities have the same appetites as our suburban brethren. Why punish us for where you choose to live?

I'll tell you what the problem is. It's Con Ed's fault: they won't tolerate any competition digging up New York's streets. There's certainly abundant evidence of how much they enjoy their monopoly.

Are there other downsides to New York life? I've barely scratched the surface. That's another one. Scratching the surface. You can't. Not without extensive damage to your nails, perhaps paws, to absolutely no effect.

Rides in the country? Furrgeddaboutit!

Opening the door and romping around the yard? Not a chance.

Opening the door and being able to take care of business right away? Not unless you live in a penthouse with a deck.

And waitin' for that damned elevator! You may not notice, but there are a lot of times our eyes are crossing by the time we finally get outside.

Now, you're probably thinking that waiting on elevators is something we'd get used to, right?

Well, yes. But. And it's a huge BUT.

That huge BUT is called Local 32B, the unionized gang of apartment workers that – this being New York City – goes on strike with regularity thus slowing down apartment living in all respects, especially the elevators.

Now you're asking what's the connection between the apartment workers and the elevators?

That's the point: there isn't any, not after that gang goes on strike. As soon as they walk out, the elevators stop working.

I know. Seems strange to you, too, doesn't it?

But it's happened every time 32B has pulled its stunt: it's also pulled the plug on elevator service. Every 2 years.

And every time I've tried calling the ASPCA to report 'em.

But guess what?

The phones aren't working either.

That 32B sure is a crappy outfit!

Thankfully, TOM and I only live on the 4th floor so the walk down isn't too long…but long enough. It certainly cuts down on the time spent choosing just the right spot, that's for sure!

City vs. Country Life

Logical but Wrong

My guess is that most of you think that dogs who live in the suburbs or the country have a much better life than those of us who live in cities. After all, it seems logical that having more space and presumably more freedom necessarily means having a more enjoyable life. So you probably think that canines and the country go together, whereas "city dogs" is a contradiction in terms, an oxymoron.

Not so. No ox in the city, and in my experience the only morons here are bipeds. Not all of them of course. But too many.

Let me tell you just some of the ways in which my life is superior because I live with concrete rather than crabgrass.

Cats and Canines

You folks think that dogs and cats are natural enemies. When confronted with a cat, we're supposed to promptly start snarling, growling, baring our fangs, raising hell and getting super-aggressive.

Similarly, cats are supposed to spit and hiss, bare their claws and be decidedly angry and equally aggressive.

After these preliminaries, you want the main event to being: full-blown fur-flying fightin' as if tearing each other apart is what we are genetically driven to do.

Well, let me fill you in on a little secret. It just 'tain't so.

Our respective DNA has nothing to do with it.

Look, forget cats for a minute. Stop and think about it. You've seen us out walking or playing in the park. We see either another dog or even another person. Some we seem to like instinctively and some we instinctively stay far away from, right? Some even prompt us to get wary, fur rising on backs, right?

Well, it's the same with some cats. Some we instinctively believe to be OK, and some not. WE can make the distinctions. It's YOU who assume that any and all cats are our natural enemies.

'Tain't so.

Now, listen carefully. Cats of course make the same distinctions we do: some dogs they discern are OK and some they believe to be decidedly not OK.

So, being a dog, I face two risks: encountering a cat I don't like and who also doesn't like me, or one who I think is OK but who doesn't think I am. In both cases, it's likely that fur can and will fly. And once fur starts flying, more grave consequences can follow.

Here's where being in the City -- ooops, The City – trumps being in the country. Out there the chances of meeting up with a hostile feline are considerably greater than here. Joyfully, being on the streets of The City reduces such risks to virtually zero.

On our outings, we don't run into cats. So the probability of being able to truly enjoy a leisurely walk versus returning home with a bloody nose is far greater in a city than in the suburbs. In all my years in The Big Apple, I've not come across a single kitty out for a walk, accompanied or otherwise.

Sure, there are cats in The City. But whereas they might roam free in the country and thus easily present themselves for confrontations, city cats, other than the feral ones and those perched on their human companions shoulders (this is New York City remember) are universally confined to their quarters. Sighting a feral feline is unheard of.

You might say being a dog in Manhattan is the cat's meow.

Cats and Koreans

Unfortunately, while that has been the general rule, it saddens me to report a major exception to this feline-free environment. Like all general rules, there is an exception. The initiative has come from abroad.

You see, just as Greeks have come to monopolize City diners, Korean fruit and vegetable stands have sprouted up on virtually every street corner in town. And here's the rub: most of these 24-

hour fresh food emporia are presided over by watch-cats.

I guess the logic is that mice and rats pose a greater threat to the inventory and therefore finances of these establishments than do starving street people and frisky teenagers. Sanitation is obviously not a consideration in any respect.

The presence of these creatures confronts TOM and me with a decidedly unpleasant difficult choice: beriberi for him or a bloody nose for me.

Talk about a paw choice...

The reason for patronizing these corner stands is because their fruit and vegetables still contain some taste and nutritional value, unlike the shoe-box sized so-called supermarkets whose merchandise – by the time it has arrived, been sorted and is delivered – lacks both.

Au Naturale Pedicures

Chances are that country canines, having mostly soft surfaces - odd things like lawns - on which to walk and romp, if and when they are permitted outside of course, have to have their nails cut. We City dogs, on the other paw, keep our nails neatly trimmed just from our daily strolls on concrete.

Now this may not sound like an important difference to you. You probably imagine that taking us for a pedicure is like taking yourself to the salon or barber shop. Well, imagine if on such an occasion, someone very much larger and stronger and whom you barely know forcibly grabs your hands and feet. Then with your limbs firmly anchored in the unyielding and none-too-gentle grip of a retired sumo-wrestler, your fingers and toes are splayed out, so that the perpetrator of your 'treatment' will have a clean shot at your nails. To perform the deed itself, your captor brings into action an instrument looking remarkably like rusty hedge-trimmers. The coup de grace is administered by a rasp last used on a rusty iron pipe.

Having put us though such torture, it's only fair that you have to pay, and pay dearly for this periodic painful process.

Me? I'll take the pedicure d'concrete paws down.

The Sweet Smells of the City

For those of us for whom interesting scents are the essence of life, an abundance of fresh air has no appeal whatsoever.

And nothing, absolutely nothing is less fresh than the streets of New York City. Not only the streets but the air above them, too. Especially on a hot, humid day, it's hard for me not to break out into a roaring rendition of "I'm in Heaven"!

Think about it: Unlike an endless string of cookie-cutter ranch houses or widely separated estates, in here every thirty feet or so there's something different. The florist is adjacent to the druggist who is bordered by the grocer next to whom is the cleaner with the hardware store abutting, then comes the pastry store with an appliance shop next door, and then - to round out only this block - the vegetable stand, one with those irksome cats.

After pausing to let vehicular traffic go through, a whole new stretch of wonders awaits, block after block after wonderfully varied urban block.

Or, if it's a residential neighborhood, there is a variety of architecture as well as smells, each home having its unique fragrant blend of its occupants and their stuff, including in many cases their pet companions.

The streets of New York are like a continuous buffet table with an endless selection of individual items. A gourmand's, or in my case a canine's delight!

And that is just the beginning. For a dog to go shopping in the 'burbs or country, it means being left behind altogether or being locked up in the family car, left alone, facing possible suffocation or theft. How much fun is that?!

Here I get to go along. I get both TOM's company and an occasional chance to help out as well. Best of all are the friendly neighborhood proprietors. After the obligatory scratching of the noggin and a hearty, "How's the little fella today?" we get down to the good stuff.

There's a pastry shop whose proprietor is the softest touch, and best baker in town, and whose cookies are to die for - if only TOM would permit more than one! Even the Chinese launderer keeps a box of dog biscuits at the ready, the contents of which are dispensed as eagerly as the clean shirts.

The pharmacist is also good for a dog biscuit or even two on a good day, 'though I keep hoping for something a bit more in his line than mine.

Contrast these receptions with the typical greeting by your friendly suburban neighbor: "Hey Mac, get your goddamned dog off my lawn!"

And the scents! Unlike left-over petroleum products on drive-ways and chemical fertilizers on lawns, the City's sidewalks and streets offer boundless and tempting odoriferous items and traces.

First of course are the markings which I and others - not all of whom, it has to be admitted, had four legs - have left behind, as it were.

Then there is the garbage. Out there, if and when it ever leaves the house, it is entombed in metal plastic bins which are hidden in a sealed off area to which we have no access. We never get so much as a distant whiff of the stuff.

Here in The City, at least on those infrequent occasions when there isn't a strike underway, everyone's garbage is at the curb, bagged and awaiting pick-up. Right out in the open. Easy access guaranteed.

Owing to the variety of establishments along the way, certainly before and even after the bags have been collected, there is a bountiful and pungent array of scents just waiting to be relished. During the summer, of course, all this gets even better, after it has had a chance to bake on its concrete oven. Tandoori Trash!

While you may think Hell is Manhattan on an August day - the third week of the perennial garbage strike - for us it's as close to

Heaven as we have any earthly right to expect. In August outside the City, we would be confined to the sanitized family room, inhaling nothing more exciting than chilled recycled air. Give me the stinking city anytime!

Audible Distractions

Among the many features that make urban living unique are city noises, their amount, level, duration and types. There are more kinds of them, more often, at higher levels, for longer periods of time, most of a more noisome nature than you are likely to find in the 'burbs much less the country.

To my surprise, I have adapted to these realities just as you seem to have, perhaps more so. Even though hearing is one of my most important and acute senses and despite the constant din, I have learned to distinguish among the plethora of loud sounds those that are only mildly irksome versus those which are truly important. Sometimes I actually do a better job at this than you do.

Here are some examples.

Let's say TOM and I are out for a stroll along Second Avenue, and we pass a construction site where demolition is underway, resulting in the need to evacuate large amounts of debris, empty-ing portable trolleys of the stuff into hyper-thyroid-sized garbage trucks or from upper levels down plastic chutes. No matter the means of making the deposit, the end result is the same: clanging and banging off the meter accompanied by enormous clouds of dust and dirt. You bipeds react in one of two ways: you either move away from the source of the noise, as if fearful of the whole mess toppling over, or you jump at each sudden BANG. In short, you react quickly and physically. Me? But I try to get closer, to check out the new scents.

Or. It's 5:30 a.m. and everyone is abed. Well, not quite every-one. The garbage-haulers, the private ones, to be sure, are a-stirring. Since this in New York City, you know it's the private haulers. How? Simple. Those on the public take, are either on strike or asleep, or both; but in no event making any noise louder than a deep snore. They don't bestir themselves until the bankers have arrived, if then.

These private sector folks are the City's equivalent of roosters crowing in the 'morn.

If you've ever wondered why Yorkers are a brusque breed, consider how their days start.

But not us. Amid all that banging n'er a single bark nor growl is heard. Not even a whimper. Like the rest of us, I'm still snoozing away peacefully even joyfully having taken over the warm spot in the bed left vacant by the screaming idiot at the window.

Here's another one: It's 10:15 p.m., and a symphony is soothing the savage beast in both of us. We're curled up in our favorite chair, TOM absorbed in his distraction, I in mine, reliving a particularly stimulating squirrel hunt, or some such. TOM is gently stroking my neck, or caressing my ear. Bliss reigns. It doesn't get much better than this.

Suddenly, screeching notes not in the score are heard. A terrible mistake by an inept amateur? The new, newer, newest wave of what used to be called music? No such luck. Rather a car alarm four floors below is doing its damnably good imitation of mechanical Whooping Cough.

Not that anyone has actually tried to steal the vehicle. Auto theft alarms are almost always set off by overly-eager parkers who have decided that the simplest way of determining clearances when maneuvering into and out of parking places is by feel rather than sight. Their touch just happens not to be especially light. It's real-life Bumper Cars.

But most car alarms are triggered by those with larceny in their hearts, entrepreneurs after radios and tape-decks, not the whole shebang speaking of bangs.

Apartment windows open and angry Yorkers start bellowing adding to the festivities.

Me? I may open one eye, but probably not.

*Yorkers being the resourceful know-it-alls of legend have taken
to posting signs in their car windows reading, "No Radio".
Those who have tried this ploy sometimes return to find their
windows smashed and a handwritten note adjacent to their own
reading, "Just checking" or - my favorite - "Get one."*

Ear Smarts

*How Pepper is able to distinguish between sounds and choose
those to which he will react and those to be ignored is a source
of wonder. As he says, the loudest, most sudden noise may not
faze him a bit. Not a muscle will move; not an ear will twitch.*

*Yet, I can be in the kitchen while he's somewhere else, perhaps
sound asleep on the sofa. I'll unwrap the cloth napkin containing
leftover bread. No sound accompanies this movement that I can
hear. Yet he appears at the kitchen door, eager for a piece of the
action.*

*Or he'll be at the other end of the apartment. The stereo is play-
ing, trying to stay a few decibels above the clamor of the city
flowing through open windows. Con Ed's jackhammer symphony
competing with Beethoven. I'm in the kitchen, banging away
with pots and pans. No dog. But let me ever so slowly and quietly
open the Saran wrapping of a piece of cheese, and somehow he
picks up that tiny crinkling sound and presents himself eagerly at
the kitchen door for his share.*

*And it's not just sounds associated with food which can produce
a reaction. When he was quite young, I was in my MASH-junkie
period, watching the nightly reruns at 11. Every night when the
show was over, I took Pepper for his last walk to empty his tanks
before bedtime.*

*This became such a routine that when the MASH theme was
played at the end of the show and as the credits began to roll,
Pepper would awaken from his nap, get up and go to the front
door, ready for his trip downstairs. He wouldn't do this when the
same music played at the beginning of the show; only at the end.*

At first I thought he was correlating the sound from the televi-

sion with his very precise biological clock, keyed to having to perform certain bodily functions at certain times of the day. Even so, I was amazed that he would respond to sounds coming from the television.

Now here's the real oddity. After this had been going on for some time, we came to a presidential election year with its attendant televised conventions. In a burst of inspired programming, the local channel that carried the MASH reruns scheduled 90 minutes of back-to-back episodes to compete with the conventions. Of course this feast took place at an earlier hour than the usual 11 p.m. reruns.

Sure enough, during a particularly boring part of the first convention, I switched to the MASH channel. At the end of each of the three episodes, when the theme-song began, Pepper bestirred himself and headed for the front door.

I can't explain it. Perhaps in his own way, he was expressing the same view of the convention that had prompted me to turn to MASH: an urge to go to the bathroom.

Aisle Be Darned

While living in a city offers me distinct advantages, I'm not certain the same is always applies to the case with TOM. Take food, for example. Not takeout, which many of you urban types appear to believe is synonymous with city living. No. Let's look at food as it was meant to be: prepared and eaten in your very own dog house, 'er home.

Elsewhere I'll talk a good bite, 'er bit, about my own food. But TOM's is another matter.

In my case, all I have to worry about is when and what I eat. For TOM his first worry is where to get it. Since I get to go along on these excursions, let me tell you what it is like.

For those of you who do not live in a city, grocery shopping is a chore you perform by getting into a station wagon, driving to an enormous warehouse, pushing a metal basket the size of a railroad car up and down dozens of aisles piled high and wide with ten different brands of every item, filling a half-dozen or more enormous paper sacks with vast quantities of foodstuffs, cramming the whole collection into the wagon, and then off-loading the goods into both the fridge upstairs and the freezer in the basement – probably forgetting to rotate the old stuff to the front. You do this once a week; and if you're really lucky, or clever, you get your spouse to do it for you.

Well, getting the goods in Manhattan is different. To begin with, virtually no one owns a vehicle of any size, and certainly not TOM. And even if you do own some wheels, what's not yet been ripped off by various teen-aged entrepreneurs is sitting cold and useless in a garage five blocks distant. But we're like most folks: In town we shop on foot. That's rule number one.

That means that rule number two is you don't buy more than you can easily carry in one or at most two small- to medium-sized shopping bags.

"Bags" in The City means thin plastic ones whose handles -mere unreinforced holes in the sides of the bags - dictate rules three and four: no sharp objects, and strictly limited weight, carefully distributed.

Those two rules mean there isn't a city dweller or grocery store check-out clerk who couldn't perform blindfolded the complicated weight and balance calculations required to get and keep even a small plane airborne.

Lumbering down the street with these knuckle-scrapers is awkward enough not to be complicated by having them rip open, scattering your goodies and smashing the ketchup bottle wide open on the pavement for the rest of the Yorker crowd to step in.

The second difference is that city markets are about the size of commemorative postage stamps. Profit margins on food being what they are and the value of urban real estate being what it is combine to produce (!) what in the food trade is called the MCMC Factor: Maximum Cramming; Minimum Comfort. MC-square. Or just MC2.

MC2 dictates that while the total number of square feet of the typical grocery store should be as low as possible, both the number of rows of shelving and their height should be as high as possible. This means that the actual aisles themselves can be comfortably and safely navigated only by professional basketball players, who are thin enough to move through them and tall enough to reach the top shelves. Sadly, with the salaries thrust upon these giants by the teams' owners, few are available to assist TOM and other mere mortals.

With shelf space so limited, there are fewer items stocked and a smaller number of brands of those items where there is a choice. Frequently this is only one brand of an item.

For the shopper, this means coming up with a blend of (a) compromising on what is eaten and/or the brand consumed and (b) the amount of time spent and number of shops visited to avoid making more compromises, always being prepared to (c) change the balance based on weather and other relevant and changing conditions, e.g. a sudden craving for a particular item or brand.

What all this means for me is that I need to be prepared for ducking into one or more grocery or other food stores almost every night on TOM's arm to fetch at least one or perhaps two bags of goodies which he'll tote in one hand while keeping hold of his end of the leash with the other end route home.

<u>Our Back Yard</u>

The Law and the Lawn

Every weekend TOM and I go to Central Park. As you might suspect, I look forward to these outings with considerable anticipation since they present several opportunities denied me, 'er us during the week.

For starters, both of us get unleashed.

Freedom indeed – not so much. You see, Pepper is quite right about the New York Leash Law: it applies in Central Park as well. Amid all the muggings and worse that are daily events in the Park, a disproportionate effort is invested in enforcing this statute, typically by mounted Park Rangers atop their trusty steeds who when spotting an unleashed dog, rush onto the scene with all the panache of a Royal Canadian Mounted Police, trumpets blaring accompanied by Nelson Eddy and Jeanette Macdonald, the horse's nostrils flaring. It's an impressive and intimidating sight.

Since I believe that dogs ought to be set free in the Park and despite a constant lookout, I get stopped too often by Rangers. The fine for an unleashed dog is $50!

After the first few tickets, during which I played it straight and gave the Ranger my real name and address, I was tipped off by another dog lover to a common scam. It's simple. Give the Ranger a fictitious name and address. Don't carry or admit to carrying any identification. And don't let the dog wear any identification either.

Since you can't be ticketed by the Rangers for failing to have proper tags for the dog, all you get for that offense is a lecture. You also get the ticket of course, but made out in the name of whichever fictional character you've provided for the occasion.

It works like a charm.

There was one time, though, when I pressed my luck a little too far. I gave the Ranger not a fictitious name and address, but the name and address of a friend in Boston, explaining that I was simply visiting for the weekend.

Several months later, I got a rather strained call from my Boston friend. What did I know about a ticket for a dog violation in Central Park for $50?!

Of course, I can enjoy this liberation only as long as I play by established rules, staying within a reasonable distance of TOM and responding to his calls with a modicum of promptness. Should I wander too far or fail to come charging back to his side when summoned, it'd be back onto the leash for certain. But as long as I mind my manners, once we leave Fifth Avenue behind, I am free and Central Park with its boundless joys is mine to explore and enjoy.

Fur Fun

As it happens, one of the Park's joys is also my own: squirrels. Owing to my ratter's heritage, I love chasing the little devils. Perhaps it's because we are the same color. Perhaps it's because, apart from the odd behavior of a lot of the two-legged beasts in the Park, they are frequently the only other animals around. Or perhaps it's because of their size. After all, if you are a miniature Schnauzer, there aren't a lot of other creatures around on whom you can look down and about whom you can feel physically superior.

In any event, I do love to chase 'em. Although I must say they don't seem to share this enthusiasm.

However the embarrassing truth is that despite my best efforts and with only one exception, I've yet to actually catch one.

I mean, I'll spot one and give chase. This is the real McCoy, what is truly meant by 'hot pursuit'. We'll be running along, never in a straight line, of course, but zig-zagging like crazy. I now know how Footballer Hirsh came by his nickname; it's an orthopedic surgeon's delight. I'll close the gap. I'll get within inches. I can begin to taste the bugger. When - whammo! - the little bastard darts behind a tree and disappears!

I race around to the back of the tree, and no squirrel. I circle and circle, but it's gone. Not a trace, and no forwarding address.

TOM, meanwhile, has stopped to observe the action. As I reappear confused and frustrated from behind the friggin' tree, he claps his hands to summons me to his side. He scruffs my ear, pats my head and tells me what a good boy I am. Which is a little hard for me to understand, since my efforts have not been to my satisfaction whatsoever. So why should my failure be cause for commendation? He's certainly not known for tolerance period, much less for tolerating failure....

I mentioned an exception. This happened a few years ago, admittedly when my step was perhaps a bit quicker. Anyway, there we were in the Park. I spotted what graduates of business schools, aka B-Schoolers, refer to as a target of opportunity' and gave chase. To my considerable delight, I actually caught it! True to my ratter's breeding, I grabbed it firmly in my jaws at the back of its neck and instinctively began to shake it furiously, with inordinate enthusiasm..........and not a little surprise.

To tell you the absolute truth, after years of having the damned things disappear behind trees, I was quite startled to suddenly find my mouth filled with a warm bundle of trembling fur.

Moreover, I gathered from its reactions that it hadn't quite expected this turn of events either.

In short, both of us were stunned.

As for TOM, well, you would have thought I had just pulled off the worst stunt ever. Stolen the crown jewels. Robbed Fort Knox. Peed on the President. Something really outrageous. I mean, his scream of my name alone was enough to curdle every cow's milk within a mile's radius. This being Central Park, the City's milk supply was safe, there not being a four-legged cow closer than the far reaches of New Jersey.

And rather than his customary stationary clapping, he came charging at us, flailing his arms and yelling his fool head off.

Now get this picture. I'm already somewhat taken aback, actually downright startled, having at long last caught a heretofore elusive prey. My chops are filled with what feels like a terrified mass of quivering hide. And to top it all off, this raving lunatic bearing no resemblance whatsoever to the calm, soothing human companion I had gotten to know and love so well, is bearing down on us, hollering and gesturing like a madman. So much for your quiet Sunday in the Park!

Have you ever been so startled that your jaw literally dropped open? Well, TOM's behavior scared the still-living quivering squirrel right out of my grip. Off it scurried, while I stood shocked still, awaiting my adored but now totally over-the-top TOM. Never in all my days had I seen him so out of control. I mean, the fierce never before seen glare in his eyes alone was enough to freeze me in my tracks.

Well, let me tell you, what with the lecture I got, the finger-shaking and the stern warnings of dire future consequences, I've made it a policy ever since not to give TOM another occasion like it. The more he ranted and raved, screamed and lectured, threatened and pleaded, the more it became clear to me that if I ever were to repeat my performance, the certain consequences would likely be graver for him than for me. I mean, if I gave him cause to react that way again, TOM might well suffer a heart attack or stroke. And no little bunch of dirty grey fur is worth it to me to run that risk.

So ever since, while I still greatly enjoy the game, and love chasing after my little furry foes, I've made it a point never to quite catch up. It just wouldn't be good for TOM's best interests...and therefore my own.

Setting aside the question of just whose health would suffer most should Pepper again succeed in catching a squirrel, his version does reveal one of his more peculiar traits.

You no doubt noted his description of where squirrels go, once they make it safely to their trees. They 'disappear' on the other side. Missing from his concept of spatial relations is any awareness of 'up'.

I'm sure you would have thought, as indeed I did, that Pepper would note the direction of his quarry's escape. The normal, textbook canine response under such circumstances would be for him to assume a posture of righteous indignation, stand on his hind legs at the base of the tree, his front legs pawing at the trunk, looking upward in the direction of escape, and barking angrily in moral outrage at the unfair and unequal turn the chase had taken, daring the squirrel to return to the field of play. Standard procedure, right? Introductory Squirrel Chasing. Freshman course. Beginner's level.

Not my beloved hunter. Absolutely not. He runs a ring or two around the base of the tree, reappears from the backside, and fixes me with an quizzical mad-as-hell expression as if to ask, "So, what have you done with the little bastard?!"

The Wild Beasts of Central Park

Frustrating as squirrels can be, they are nothing next to the real beasts that inhabit Central Park.

TOM and I are strolling in the Park. That is, he is strolling the path; I'm romping over the lawns. Both of us are reveling in Nature and the exquisite freedom of not being leashed. Let's say it's one of those picture-perfect spring or fall days when New York simply sparkles. In short, Heaven!

Into this bliss from the opposite direction appears a young couple with their even younger child, old enough to be upright and stumbling under his own power yet not quite fully coordinated or in complete control of most other bodily functions.

Fearful of what TOM may do during the coming encounter, I promptly return to his side just in case.

As the gap closes, Daddy or Mommy inevitably coos to Baby, "Look, Justin, a Bow-Wow." At this point, TOM, who's not too fond of little people or indulgent parents to begin with, murmurs under his breath something like, "No, you idiots, it's a goddamn giraffe!"

We have now closed to within a few paces; and Mommy - I don't know why it's always Mommy perhaps because Daddy feels it would be beneath his pin-striped dignity - looks at TOM and asks demurely, "Can he pet him?"

Given TOM's attitude, and I do mean 'attitude', I always expect him to say, "It's okay with me, Lady; but you should know the dog is rabid."

Instead, to my utter surprise he politely says, "Sure", bends down, grabs my collar making my escape impossible, and actually invites The Kid to approach. Truth is I think it's his secret hope that I'll bite the little sucker's nose or any other conveniently protruding body part.

Typically, the Future President, national or at least corporate, whose deportment was impeccable during his recent admissions interview for the one pre-school program in New York that absolutely guarantees his acceptance by Harvard, after taking his cue from Mommy, now makes a grab for my nose with one hand while simultaneously madly waving the other about my head.

In a fit of ecstatic discovery that his academically hypersensitive parents construe as a definitive indication of intellectual promise, his blond, blue-eyed head not six inches from my own, the little fucker SCREAMS BLOODY MURDER!

Do I jump? Do I bolt? Do I snarl? Bare my teeth? Rise up on my hind legs, tower over him and glare? Do I do what any sane creature should do, faced with such provocation? Bite the little shit on those sticky little fingers, or anyplace else I can quickly reach?

Absolutely not. I remain totally controlled. Stoic. The very picture of patience and inter-species tolerance and understanding. I simply drop my rump, sit on the invariably cold, damp pavement, and glance pleadingly up at TOM: "Get me the hell outta here!"

Meanwhile Mommy and Daddy are busy congratulating their Pride and Joy on his courage and bravery - which seems to me a bit excessive as well as misplaced since I rather think my performance the more meritorious. TOM smiles indulgently at them, glances down at me and urges me to move along, saying for all to hear, "What a good boy!"

You know what? I bet those dolts think TOM is talking about

their Super Brat.

If I'm lucky, I'll have escaped from this zoological encounter with eyes and ears still intact and no more damage than a patch of sticky fur somewhere aft of my delicate nose. Even little people fresh from a bath have sticky fingers. Heaven alone knows how that can be.

Grooming Groans

Hellcuts

One of my least favorite outings is being taken, very much against my will, for a hellcut. TOM calls it 'grooming', but since he doesn't have to endure it, he can call it anything he wants. To me, it's living hell.

Not only does he not go through it himself, he actually has the gall to leave the premises after depositing me into the clutches of one of these sadists, so that I have to endure the forthcoming torture totally alone. If he doesn't have to hang around, why should I?

You probably can't imagine what the problem is. After all, you seem to take yourself to your groomer voluntarily, more often, and with what looks very much like pleasurable anticipation. Right?

From what I can see, I can understand why your experience is different from mine.

In TOM's case, he's in and out in a half-hour at the most. Women I've known take considerably longer probably because they have a lot more hair than TOM does.

And in both cases, only the tops of your heads get 'groomed'.

I'm not nearly as lucky. In my case, it's a full-body job, not even excluding my most private parts.

Think about it. How would you feel if you were dragged from the comfort of your own home, then abandoned by your beloved companion, placed in a small cage only to be later taken forcibly against your will, completely submerged in tepid water, scrubbed within an inch of your life, hauled out and smothered with a towel that rubs you abrasively all over?

Then under the untender care of a total stranger, you find yourself chained to a scaffold while a Minister of Mowing, a Corporeal Cropper, a Barbarous Barber first fries you with blasts from a portable hot air furnace and, for finishing touches, attacks your entire body with very sharp shears and scissors? Comes right at your eyes, ears, stomach, your back, your neck, legs, and yes, even your privates. All this while you're still chained to that damned scaffold.

Where are the protections of the Geneva Conventions? Where's the ASPCA? WHERE'S TOM?!?!?!!?

AND, having barely – and take that quite literally – survived, you are rewarded by being returned to another small cage where you are left to shiver and suffer all alone, save for other brutalized pups going through their own hell.

In any civilized society this is called bondage, torture, even cruel and inhuman for you and banned by those Conventions and subject to very harsh penalties – but no, not for us.

Why the hell not?!?!?!

Pepper hates being groomed, as you may have gathered. I hear from time to time of dogs who, according to their human companions at least, actually like the experience. Some even claim that their pets will primp after being groomed. Well maybe so. But Pepper's feelings on this topic are unambiguously negative.

So much so that even years later he still will not turn the corner and walk with me down the street where he was first taken to be groomed as a puppy. Try to head that way and as soon as he nears that corner, he bolts to the far side of the sidewalk and tries to pull further away, tugging on his leash as if he were possessed.

And it's not just that place. I've tried a succession of groomers, hoping that it is the person and not the experience to which he takes such obvious exception. But his reaction is consistent. After the first visit, I can barely get him to stay on the sidewalk even if we're just walking past the place. He heads for the curb and bolts past the doorway as fast as his legs and mine are willing to go.

Speaking of a first grooming, in fairness I should share my own reaction to Pepper's first trip to a groomer.

Just as Pepper described it, I simply dropped him off and went on to work. When I returned at the end of the day to pick him up, I paid the groomer who then disappeared into the back of the store.

The next thing I knew some strange, little, and I do mean little, grey animal came dashing up to me. For more than just a flashing moment, I didn't make the connection. I didn't recognize or even think it was Pepper.

I don't know what I had expected. I don't really think I had thought about it at all in fact. I dropped off Pepper and expected to pick up Pepper when I returned.

But this bald, funny-looking, tiny thing? Whose was it? What was it?

Standing there stunned and confused, I actually thought that maybe the groomer had made a mistake and was giving me the wrong dog. I even thought, if you can believe this, that maybe it wasn't a mistake and the groomer was deliberately trying to make a switch. I know that must sound crazy, but this was New York after all. Even so....

Can you imagine what must have been going through Pepper's mind? After the day he'd had? Literally jumping for joy at my feet. And what does he get in return? I'm all but backing away.

And who knows what the groomer must have been thinking during all this? Maybe he'd seen such a dumbfounded, I mean really stupid, reaction before. I certainly hope so.

To this day I don't know which was the greater shock: that Pepper looked so completely different or that I hadn't recognized my own dog.

Haunts me to this very day.

Cut the Cropping

Which brings me to another, more serious form of trimming. Awful as the cosmetic grooming is, it is nothing next to the cropping of our ears and tails.

Listen up. I'm being serious now. Cutting off pieces of ears and tails is not, may I repeat not!, natural. It is not nice. And it hurts like hell.

I know, you claim it doesn't hurt. Well I promise you this: those who tell you that it doesn't hurt have never had it done to them. And if you don't believe me, try it on yourself. Forget the poking of a tiny hole in your ear lobe. Cut off a chunk of your ear and see how you like it.

Better yet, whack off most of your tail bone, which in your case means prior removal of some butt. But who cares?

You're damn right who cares: it hurts like hell, doesn't it?!

Compounding this miserable maiming, you have it done when we are very, very young. If the howling of a baby boy having his foreskin cut doesn't curdle your blood and make you feel guilt, imagine cutting off some of the little dear's ears and/or butt.

You'd be arresting for child abuse and worse, and rightfully so.

But go ahead and whack away at us with abandon, all in the sole interest of making us look like something you want us to look like. Never mind the trauma to us.

Makes us dog-gone mad and I mean MAD.

Besides, we're supposed to be your best friends. Is chopping off parts of our bodies, inflicting such traumas on us as babies any way to treat what are destined to become beloved family members?

Besides, what other animals do you so consistently maim to conform to your preconceived ideas of what they should look like? Cats? Horses? Gerbils? Pigs?

Why us?

You do understand that having the ASPCA and the AKC side-by-side is the height of hypocrisy, don't you?

So do us and yourselves a favor: cut out the cropping. Love us for who we are naturally.

Either that or give us an opportunity to share in the fun by maiming you to fit our idealized versions of you!

For Whom the Groomer Toils

And another thing while we're on the subject.

I do understand, I'm not saying I agree, but I do understand that periodic baths are probably in our shared best interests, yours and ours.

After all we do share the same space, sealed in together in some cases year 'round while only during the coldest of winters for others. Furthermore, we allow some of you to share beds we have commandeered, while others of us prefer, or are required, to sleep alone.

Almost all of you bathe or shower daily, what to us is the just the first of a series of things you do. Another is brushing your teeth. Yet another is applying stuff to your body that smells funny.

Based solely on my experience with what TOM smells like when he comes back from his run versus after he has completed his shower-brushing-spraying, I for one greatly appreciate the effort.

I assure you this is not unappreciated given the sensitivity of our noses. So I guess periodic baths are not unreasonable for us to endure.

Some of you undertake to bathe us at home, which – to be frank - is almost always a mixed blessing: we are spared a trip to the dreaded groomers but subjected to the ministrations of amateurs: well-intended but mostly inept, e.g. you never take proper care of our ears. No surprise given the ones you are used to. Take it from us: best to stick to your day jobs.

But most of you rely on your neighborhood groomers to under-take not only the bathing but also the grooming.

And that's where the serious trouble begins. The bathing part is bad enough as I've just told you. But the worst is what comes after the bath: what you call 'grooming' but what we call Hell on Earth.

That such torture is instigated by those we hold most dear, that's what cuts the most.

Because we know – and worse, we know you know – that how

we are groomed is entirely for your benefit and most certainly not ours.

Think about it. In my case, you think we were born with a natural Schnauzer cut: virtually bare all over except for whiskers and legs?! It may look cool to you but its friggin' freezing or broiling to me. How would you like to go through life bald all over?!

Pepper came to live with us in the summer. When winter was approaching, I asked our vet whether we should put a sweater on him in cold weather. His response? "It won't make much difference to him but it'll make you feel better."

So we got Pepper a couple of sweaters and forced him into one when the weather got cold. And I do mean 'forced', as the Tiny Terror was none too happy to be confined.

So one winter Saturday we did not put a sweater on him before heading out to Central Park for our walk. Despite romping free in his untethered explorations of the Park, after about a half hour he started shivering. And I do mean full-body shivering.

We scooped him up, wrapped him in one of our scarfs, bolted to the nearest exit, got a cab not-soon-enough, tucked him under my coat on the ride home and made sure the radiators were on full blast after getting him home.

Eventually the shivering stopped and he went to sleep.

He never went out without a sweater in cold weather again.

Let me ask you this: What dimwit decided that a poodle should look like that? I mean, a Schnauzer cut is bad enough; but a poodle's?! It's gives new meaning to demeaning and disrespect. It's a crime against Nature. And it's entirely for your benefit, not Fifi's.

Why do you go along with this nonsense? Do you think for one minute it makes the least bit of difference to us? Do you actually believe that we care what we look like? Do you imagine us liking or disliking another dog just because of its haircut? "I'm not going to play with Gretchen until she has a proper poodle trim." Get real!

And why do some of us even have 'cuts' and not others? Does a boxer? A dachshund?

I suspect it's the AKC again and its members: all those who have a financial stake in creating and maintaining distinctions more in their interests than in Nature's own. Shame on them.

Groom with a View

For reasons passing understanding, TOM decided early on that I should be abused, 'er brushed every night. I don't know whether this is because he showers every day and figures I should have the equivalent; if it's his way of making certain there are no snags in my coat; or if it's just that he wants to inflict a daily dosage of discomfort. Whatever the reason, beginning when I was just a pup, I have had to endure this nightly brutality.

While on the surface, as it were, this may not strike you as a reason to complain, please note that the instrument of torture is a wire brush. This means it is regrettably very effective at finding snags in my hair - and you know what that feels like – while it's sharp points run across the surface of my skin. Make your skin crawl too?!

At first, to lure me into being subjected to this abuse TOM would pick out a favorite toy, hoping I would be so pleased to play with it that I wouldn't notice or care overly much about being scoured with that damned brush. My brain may be small, but my pain-avoidance instinct is acute.

Naturally I tried to escape every night. TOM would grab me. I fought back. He would tighten his grip. I squirmed. He yanked me back. I twisted and turned some more. He yanked some more. Of course, he could only yank with one hand, since the other was wrapped around the brush, which he'd try to apply to my frantic wiggling frame. My hope was to make the experience as painful and unpleasant for him as for me.

What with my Teutonic stubbornness matching his, the nightly battle was never brief. I can't imagine he enjoyed these tugs of war and will any more than I did.

After a year or so of this nightly nonsense, I regret to report that TOM had a stroke of something more than that damned brush. He solved his problem by creating an insurmountable one for me. How? He changed the venue from the floor to a table top!

By moving the site of the torture to an elevated one, he cut off any convenient means for me to escape. Sure, I could continue to struggle and resist. But if I did manage to break free, that might not be all that got broken in the process. I mean, cats can take confidence in always being able to land on their feet. As far as I know, dogs don't share that ability. I know I certainly didn't want to find out.

Let me put it this way. I don't feel comfortable jumping off anything I haven't been able to jump onto. It's a classic case of pride going before a fall. By putting me on a table the height of which is beyond my jumping zone, TOM automatically made it virtually impossible for me to escape. I mean, what's a mere wire brush next to snapped bones or a smashed nose?

The best I can do is try to avoid getting caught in the first place. But, fast as I am, in a small apartment with doors that can be shut in every room, I can run but I cannot hide. There's no avoiding ultimate capture. Hoisted thus against my will, I have no choice but to quiet down and take my nightly medicine.

On the other hand, the alternative to nightly brushings would be more frequent baths. Baths so far as I am concerned are to be avoided at all costs: the ultimate indignity and discomfort. If you think we look like the saddest of puppies you ever saw when drenched and shivering, it's because at least I feel exactly the way I look: miserable.

You know what having a bath is to me? Canine waterboarding – the ultimate, and immoral if not illegal, torture. Brutality at its beastly best.

So with that prospect as a deterrent as well as the height, I've had no choice but to tolerate TOM and his prickly, painful brush.

Presumably riddled with guilt, when it is all over TOM 'rewards' me with a disproportionately tiny snack. I assure you, the reward does not come close to fitting the crime.

When he reaches down to hand me my incredibly small treat, I attack it with such enthusiasm that I always make sure to grab for a little more than just the midget morsel.

Since my teeth and his flesh meet often, I don't feel completely vanquished.

<u>Travel Time</u>

First Fright, er, Flight

I was almost two years old when I took my first airplane ride. The occasion was a family vacation on a small island off the Georgia coast. To get there meant flying from New York to Jacksonville, Florida, and then driving back north to Jekyll Island.

This was not going to be my first extended trip out of New York City, however. Nope, well-traveled pup that I am, I had already been to Cape Cod.

We had gone to the Cape for my first summer vacation mainly because it was possible to drive there from Manhattan, which made taking me along easy. I guess I was sufficiently convincing on that trip that I was on friendly enough terms with sand that another similar venue was feasible. And while I had already demonstrated that I was an acceptable automobile traveler, all bets were off when it came to getting on an airplane.

Long before final plans were laid, there had been extended discussions at home as to whether such an adventure made sense or whether the smart thing to do would be to return to Cape Cod.

As part of their research TOM and Bonnie learned that the airlines offered two choices. One option was that I could go in the belly of the plane just like the rest of the baggage. The other option depended on whether I could fit into a portable carrier that would itself fit under an airline seat. If so I could accompany them in the cabin.

Important as the issue was especially to me, I was neither consulted nor given a vote. This did not improve my already skeptical feelings about an airplane ride. You may recall my less than pleasant prior experience with small cages; I know I do. Too well.

TOM and Bonnie decided, wisely, to try for the in-cabin option. They focused on two questions: Would I fit into a carrier? And if so, how would I behave?

The first was easily determined, after a fashion that is. TOM measured my height and width, went wherever he went, and apparently concluding that I could fit, came home with what I assumed was the container into which I was to be placed. It seemed kind of small to me, and I sniffed, circled and checked it out. As I did so, it kept getting smaller and smaller while my considerable eyebrows kept rising and my less considerable tail kept drooping.

Suffice to say the prospect of being entombed in this crate became so frightening that I lost all perspective totaling forgetting that the alternatives were to be stuck in with the baggage or, worse, left behind. I decided that passive civil resistance would be insufficient. Active resistance was called for, fear being the motivator it can be.

TOM and Bonnie spent one night trying to entice, goad, tug, haul, urge, prod, bribe, induce, seduce, persuade, and/or propel me into that thing.

The end result: all three of us were well spent and still they did not know if I could fit and I did not want to find out. What to them was a goal to be achieved was to me a gaol to be avoided.

So the next night, TOM tried holding me still while Bonnie tried maneuvering the crate over top of me. I may be small, but I can squirm mightily when I put my mind to it; and I assure you, by this time my mind was indeed focused on staying out of that damned crate.

By the third night, TOM – clearly frustrated and borderline mad - had Bonnie hold the top of the crate open, picked me up, and literally crammed me in. Even with all four limbs flailing wildly and body wiggling with the outright fear, TOM – who after all slightly outclassed me in strength, reach and in this case even determination - prevailed. In relatively short order, I found myself encased in a space decidedly less than a tourist class seat.

Turning around was out of the question. Both my tush and my nose were in firm contact with the ends of the gaol. Standing, my spine was developing an intimate relationship with its top. Trying to lie down was an exercise in contortionism. The only way it was possible was to scrunch down into as small a package as possible with all four limbs tucked underneath. My worst fear became developing an itch.

As if the space wasn't bad enough, the floor and sides were hard plastic, broken only by two tiny holes at each end. Half the top was the same, with the other half being finely woven metal screening, meaning my discomfiture would be on ready display for anyone caring enough to notice. There wasn't even room enough to lift my head to stare angrily back at the brutes. Bottom-line: there was absolutely no wiggle room. Literally.

Since it had now been demonstrated that I could make the trip in the cabin but that it was going to be something of a struggle with a decidedly uncooperative passenger, TOM and Bonnie began to wonder whether anything could be done to ease my fears. The vet suggested giving me a tranquilizer.

When departure day arrived, shortly before leaving the apartment, TOM pried open my mouth and popped the tranquilizer down my gullet. In fact, I may not have been the only one medicated that day. By the time we got to Kennedy Airport, I was feeling rather spacy mentally if not physically, and frankly nothing else, off on my own trip long before the plane ever left the ground.

I never could figure out whether sending me on my own flight without any means of propulsion was for my benefit or theirs. Either way, I ended up with concurrent highs.

So there we were, the three of us, ensconced in a metal tube, TOM and Bonnie in their seats, and me in the cage on the floor under the seat in front. At least, that's where I began the flight.

But it wasn't long before a combination of my pleading if somewhat unfocused eyes and TOM's guilt worked their magic, and the cage and I were elevated to TOM's lap. He even opened the top so they could stroke my back, pat my head, scratch my ears...in short, to try to make nice.

Had I been my unmedicated self, at the first slight opening of the lid no doubt I would have bounded out and up the aisle. But since I had already become a chartered member of the Mile High Club, I was content to be content, just as long as the top wasn't closed again and I got shoved back under that odorous seat.

I'm not certain how long either trip lasted. Most of me had begun to feel that the flights were endless, which in my state, seemed like a really good thing.

But not all of me felt that way. One part had begun to develop a strong desire to find a fire hydrant. A tree. A lamp-post. A mail box. Even a leg. Anything vertical.

My eyes which up to this point had been unfocused now began to cross.

I was beginning to understand what the pilot meant when he talked about a pressurized cabin. The cabin wasn't the only object under pressure at that point.

Just when I figured matters were about to get out of at least my control, I heard the sweetest words I think I have ever heard: "Ladies and gentlemen, we are beginning our descent into Jacksonville." Had my legs not been firmly squished against my undercarriage, adding to the pressurization of course, I would have jumped for joy. I was heartened to know that I was soon going to be able to dampen something other than my own spirits. The only remaining question was which would pop first during the descent: my ears or my bladder?

What I am happy to tell you is that the good folks in Jacksonville certainly have their priorities straight and in upright order. Immediately outside of their baggage claim area is a blessed spot, a 'Rest Stop for Dogs' read the sign.

Closer than cabs, parking spaces, shuttle busses to rental cars, nearer to the exit than anything else is a plot of turf from which sprouts the loveliest profusion of vertical items in Christendom. Trees. Posts. Fire hydrants. Benches. Poles. All plastic imitations, mind you; but functional nonetheless.

Amid thousands of acres of concrete is this one small plot of real soil whose only purpose in life is to provide precisely the opportunity I so badly needed.

Well, I wasted no time. All TOM had to do was pop open the top of that cage and I staggered straight to the nearest upright object.

No point in sniffing around for the best place. By this time, the best place was the nearest place. It seemed to me, in my still somewhat loopy state, that I stood there longer than the flight itself.

It was a sight I won't soon forget.

Poor Pepper. Badly as he needed that post and as urgent as his certain need, he was still feeling some of the influence of the tranquilizer. The combination of the medication and of having been penned in his cage for several hours meant that his gait was at best uncertain and none too steady. He staggered over to that post, lifted his leg, and then leaned weakly against it. He looked for all the world like a classic drunk, with a limb clinging to the post for support.

And the longer he stood there, the funnier it got. I mean he stood there, and stood there, and stood there. Never before and certainly never since have I seen my little miniature Schnauzer, or any other dog for that matter, spend so long attending to such matters and obviously needing to do so.

I don't know how much of it was the remaining tranquilizer or being weakened from his most recent efforts, but when he finally let go of that post and turned to wobble back to where I was waiting, that was one spent puppy. I mean dog tired.

TOM'S Travels and My Travails

There came a time when TOM's job took him out of town with some frequency. At first it was for relatively brief periods of time, a few days to maybe a week. Then, the trips got longer, two or more weeks. There was even one summer when he disappeared for a full month. He was on the road about a third of the time.

Fine. He'd be off having a wonderful time, I guess. At least, I assume he enjoyed it; he did it so often. But what about me?

Happily, TOM never sent me away to live with complete strangers. Nor did he ever send me to be confined in some awful commune, aka a boarding kennel. The stories I heard about such places from pals I'd meet on the street were truly frightening.

We went through several phases. The first phase was when he made arrangements for someone to come and stay with me in our, or under those circumstances, my apartment.

That was a lot of fun, and came with benefits: I was part of the interviewing process and consulted on the decision; the supervision was less and typically I got more treats. Sometimes the sitter's food was better than TOM's, pizza for example.

The process worked this way. TOM would invite the prospective sitter to the apartment to be interviewed for the job: and to see how whoever the she was - it was always a she- and I would get along. If for some reason I didn't like a particular candidate, I'd have nothing to do with her. On the other hand, if I liked one, I'd be in her lap, happily licking a lobe.

As luck would have it, not too long after beginning the search, we found a really super sitter, Susan. Irish to the core, this lovely young, and I do mean young, lady seemed to live to make me happy. I tell you, when she was on the job, I hardly missed TOM.

And she was on the job a lot in those days. There were even times her mom would come in from Long Island and stay with us in the apartment. Being pampered by two charming women is not all that bad. TOM who?

But alas, all good things must end eventually; and Susan's personal life got to where she was no longer able to come for our extended visits together.

Then, TOM and I fell into the delightful arms of a retired lady who lived around the corner and who regularly supplemented her Social Security by taking in one dog at a time as a temporary boarder. Being in the middle of Manhattan, she had a thriving little business. She was recommended to TOM by his friend the Flower Shop Lady and to me by her mink-wrapped poodle Melina, the Hooker of Second Avenue.

This wonderful woman is not only kindness personified, but,

unlike Susan, she is home all day. Talk about attention. And does she know how to spoil me! I tell you, it only took one visit before it was, "Susan; who's Susan?" Doris is her name and no temporarily orphaned animal ever had better, more loving, devoted care. I enjoyed her loving attention for quite a while.

Then two concurrent developments prompted a major change in this happy pattern. TOM's trips got to be far more frequent as well as longer. With Doris's thriving business, she was no longer a dependable solution. But in a stroke of exceeding good fortune, Bonnie, with whom, after all, I had shared the first several years of my life, became available to care for me.

So began what came to be a frequent routine. One night, TOM would pull out his suitcase, which I soon learned meant that mine would not be far behind. Sure enough, the next night after dinner instead of our extended walk, we'd only take a short spin before returning to the apartment. Rather than heading out for the evening, TOM headed for the special place where my suitcase was stashed. Right away, I knew what was up.

After stuffing it with the necessary provisions (food, toys, coat if wintertime, brush, and medicine), it would be out the door and into a cab for the long ride up and across town to Bonnie's apartment.

While I was saddened to see TOM's suitcase appear, I have to say in all candor that I was always happy to see mine, since I had a wonderful time at Bonnie's. So much so that I got to looking forward to what I had come to think of as camping out.

Not that life on Upper West End Avenue was primitive. But Bonnie's life style and her way of caring for me were different from TOM's. Feminine. More indulgent. Less rigorous. Softer. I didn't get attacked by that damned brush every night. More treats! If TOM had to be away, Bonnie's place and care were more than suitable. A nice change, and welcome variety.

Indeed, the arrangements were always so pleasant, that I hardly minded TOM's frequent absences. And you know something else? It was nice having the three of us together again, even if only for those brief periods of dropping off and picking up.

Pepper, his various sitters, and his adjustments to temporary arrangements have been interesting to observe over the years.

Susan, for example. On one of my first extended trips when she was taking care of Pepper and I being the nervous parent, I called from Caracas, Venezuela to see how things were going. Susan reported that everything was just fine, Pepper was perfectly okay, but that apparently she was a restless sleeper.

At first, I couldn't quite grasp the relevance of this piece of news, or why it was something I needed or wanted to know. Then she explained. She said that Pepper went to bed with her to go to sleep; but that the next morning, she'd find him out on the living room sofa!

I promised, at her urging, never to reveal this to her boyfriend.

Or the lady who only sat Pepper once, at the very beginning. I no longer remember why I didn't use her again. Totally forgot about her, in fact.

Then several years later, Pepper and I were strolling up Second Avenue after dinner when all of a sudden, he damn near yanked my arm off and headed back from where we'd just passed. Naturally I turned to see what had so captured his attention. He was literally jumping for joy, bouncing up and down on his rear legs, yelping with glee in the arms of some strange lady.

Well, I certainly hadn't recognized her. But Pepper had. She explained who she was. Yup, that long-ago sitter.

It was then that I began to suspect that Pepper was apparently enjoying my trips more than I was!

As for his trips to Bonnie's, it is uncanny. He knows exactly when the cab has reached Broadway, crossing from the East to the West Side, en route to her West End Avenue apartment.

Once settled in the cab leaving our apartment, Pepper will curl up in my lap, quietly enduring the ride the length of which depends on traffic and weather. But as soon as the cab hits Broadway, whether stopping for a light or moving right along, he'll stand up, put his front paws on the side window, and start happily whimpering.

He doesn't do this at Amsterdam or Columbus Avenues. If we cross over in mid-town and head north on the west side, he doesn't do it at all, not even when we finally reach Bonnie's apartment. No, we have to cross Broadway somewhere north of mid-town. Then, no matter where we make the crossing, his reaction is the same. Barely contained excitement.

Sitters aside, it's interesting how widely different our reactions are to my travels now that he goes to stay with Bonnie. All that needs to happen is for his suitcase to appear to set off rounds of gleeful yipping and yelping, mad crashing around the house, jumping onto the furniture with great abandon, and the ultimate sign of eagerness: hopping up and down nipping at my back side, urging me to get a move on. I know it's the ultimate sign as he does the same damn jumping and nipping while waiting for the elevator after I've asked him if he wants to go to the park.

That nipping is only one reason why I think of him often during long flights.

I, on the other hand, go through terrible separation anxiety for days leading up to my departure. My worry is that "something will happen" to Pepper, that I will lose him and thus not only suffer his loss but also have to endure my guilt for having brought it about.

Curiously, my fears are rarely that something will happen to me, and that Pepper will be the one to suffer and mourn my loss.

Perhaps it is because I know he is with Bonnie that I don't worry about his life should anything happen to me.

While I am away, there appear to be similarly different reactions. From all reports Pepper shows no signs of missing me, being entirely happy and content with his sitter at our home or with Bonnie at her home.

On the other hand, I miss him terribly. There are times when the ache is palpable. Especially late at night, after concluding the activity of the day and finally being left alone by my over-solicitous hosts, when Pepper and I would be cuddling together in bed after the lights were out and just before drifting off to sleep, when he would be cradled in my arms and tucked under my chin, in the darkness of countless hotel rooms I have talked to him, missed him and wept for him or more likely for myself. Lumpy hotel pillows are no real substitute.

While our reactions before and during my absences are quite different, it pleases me greatly to report how similar they are upon my return. As excited and happy as Pepper was at the departure point, his unrestrained joy on my return knows no bounds. The jumping, the yelping, the happy whimpers, the licking, the burrowing into my lap, the racing around and jumping back into my arms, and ultimately the exquisitely deep sigh when finally at rest cradled in my arms – all this is matched fully if somewhat less demonstrably by my own utter and complete relief and contentedness to once again be together.

I guess in the last analysis, that's it. While apart, it feels to me like an important and essential part of my being is missing; I feel fragmented, incomplete, uneasy. Whereas when we are rejoined together once more, I feel whole, complete, restored. I feel at peace.

It hurts like hell to leave. It is a joy to come home.

<u>Summer Vacations</u>

Headin' South

Remember that flight I was telling you about to Jacksonville, Florida? As I mentioned, it was the first leg of our trip to Jekyll Island, Georgia.

Before Bonnie and TOM split up, that's where the three of us used to vacation, Jekyll Island, a sand spit just south of Sea Island. We'd have either a cottage or a hotel room right on the beach, and spend lots of time simply wandering around.

That was where they first tried to induce me into the ocean. When we'd gone to Cape Cod our cottage apparently hadn't been near enough to the ocean or something. Anyway, I say 'induce' for two reasons. First, I am not overly fond of bodies of water larger than my drinking bowl. Second, if I used the more descriptive and, frankly, accurate word for their efforts, they'd likely be arrested by the SPCA.

Let's face it. From where I stand, looking out at an ocean is definitely not an appealing prospect. If you doubt this, go to the edge of the water, get down on your belly, lift your head six inches and see for yourself.

It looks awfully big. The waves alone are monstrous looking, overwhelmingly threatening!

It soon became clear why they had picked such a deserted island with hardly anyone else around. Picture the scene. Two adult human beings standing knee deep in the water, facing shore, and beckoning, calling, pleading, cajoling, waving arms, shouting, gesturing, semaphoring, beating the water, seemingly having lost all control of their faculties....all trying to get 14 pounds of frightened, quivering fur to join them.

If the water alone wasn't a scary enough sight, imagine what the two of them looked like! I mean, if that's what being in the water did to you, there was no way on earth I was going to have any part of it. It confirmed my view that water's fit for being in a bowl and little else.

But that little waterfront scene was only the beginning of what they had in mind for my 'holiday'.

You see, they had rented a car to get us from the Jacksonville airport back north to Jekyll and to have for getting around while on the Island and for important matters, like buying food. What could be more important than that?!

Well, after a lovely al fresco dinner on our patio facing the ocean – safely at a distance - and a little walk, we would pile into the car for a spin around the Island. Except they had in mind something more than a leisurely after dinner drive.

May I remind you that I am a miniature Schnauzer. As you know, we were bred to catch vermin around the farm. Which means that going after little furry creatures is in our genes. No amount of lazing around a comfy New York apartment erased this genetic predisposition, as you may have noted in an earlier chapter.

Do you know what the dominant population is of certain southern coastal islands? I'll tell you what. Wild rabbits!

I discovered this not long after our first arrival on the Island. While out checking the grounds, I ran across what proved to be an endless supply of these hoppy, er, happy little critters.

Unlike their domesticated cousins up north who have grown accustomed to having us around, wild rabbits instinctively dash away at the first hint, sight, scent or sound of me. And unlike squirrels with whom I can have an almost-even foot race, I'm no match for wild rabbits who don't really play fair.

Oh, they do run fast enough all right. But in addition, they have this really annoying capability of leaping tall buildings in a single bound. Well, okay, not buildings, but bushes, trees, undergrowth, anything that seems to lie between me and their escape. In short, as I am, I am sorely disadvantaged.

Here's where Bonnie and TOM came to the rescue, kind of.

While wild rabbits would run like hell if they saw, heard or smelled me coming, they had gotten used to vehicular traffic on their island. Whereas I couldn't get close enough on my own to give chase before they would hurriedly depart the scene, they thought nothing of continuing to munch away on some roadside delicacies while cars went past.

If you see what's coming, they didn't. Here's how those alleg-edly leisurely after-dinner drives were spent. With either Bonnie or TOM behind the wheel, the other would hold me on his or her lap, perched so that I could see out the side window. They would mosey the car along one of the Island's roads until they saw a rabbit having its roadside dinner. They would ease the car up next to it, by which time even I had caught sight of my quarry, triggering all kinds of thrashing and barking, at which point the door would be opened and the chase would be on!

Between the warning of the door's opening and their competitive edge, the damned rabbits always got away.

Bonnie and TOM would become convulsed with mirth while I got frustrated and mad as hell. This little game gave a whole new definition to the meaning of a 'road show'.

If the scene on the beach looked silly, imagine what the even-ing's entertainment must have looked like.

No wonder they had picked such a deserted place. In their eager-ness to avoid embarrassment, I do wish they had spared me mine as well.

Well, that's his version. But did you notice that he didn't say that he found any of this so distasteful that he refused to go along? The fact is he was the first one to the car after dinner, racing up to it and jumping wildly at the door, clearly eager to get under-way. However preposterous and silly it may have looked...and been....his enthusiasm for the evening's entertainment certainly seemed genuine at the time.

And maybe it was just my imagination, but I swear I thought I detected a slight grin on his face as he drifted off to a nap once back to the cottage and warmed by the gas fire against the chilly summer breeze.

Headin' North

After Bonnie and TOM split up, and after TOM began his

extensive travels, most of my holidays have been spent in Manhattan, except for two wonderful exceptions.

Twice TOM and I spent our summer holiday in New Hampshire where TOM's best friend, Warren, lived. Each year Warren found us a cottage to rent, the first year on Lake Winnipesaukee and the next year on Crescent Lake, where we camped out for three glorious weeks each. Well, not camped out as in tents. Nope, no way. TOM and I enjoyed our comforts. Small cottages suited us just fine.

Simply put, it was heaven on earth! To begin with, TOM was around all the time. Then, there we'd be, amid beautiful, glorious surroundings. Lots of peace and quiet. Warm days. Cool nights. Plenty of dirt roads and woodsy trails. New scents galore. Leisure time to wander aimlessly, exploring everything casually and carefully.

Except when we went into town, I never had to be on a leash, freeing both of us to enjoy completely our extended walks morning, afternoon, and night. More fresh air and exercise than imaginable. Plenty of good food, exercise, endless explorations and new scents and quiet afternoon naps. In short, all that I could ever possibly hope for.... except a fourth week!

Our daily routine was full of fun and hardly strenuous. We'd sleep a little later, but not much, since we both wanted to be up to enjoy the cool, crisp early morning.

After a leisurely breakfast on the porch overlooking the lake, we'd take off on an hour's hike, exploring the lake shore: one direction one day, then the opposite direction the next and the middle one on day 3. Repeat the cycle, again and again.

By mid-morning we'd return to the cottage, hop into the car, and dash into town for the New York paper and a loaf of freshly-baked bread. We would swing by Warren's office and, if his schedule permitted, sit a spell on a little bench out front, watching the world and the tourists go by.

Back to the cottage for lunch on the porch, then adjourn to the little dock at waterside for tea and fruit. TOM brought along whatever he was reading. I'd be content to be either curled up in his lap getting my back stroked or stretched out on the dock, feeling the warming rays of the sun while listening to the gentle lapping of the small waves against the pilings. It wasn't long before both of us were into some serious Z's.

By mid-afternoon, we would bestir ourselves and stretch our legs a bit along the lake shore. TOM then changed for his daily run, when I would be confined to the cottage to doze fitfully until he returned an hour later. Fortunately he always got himself cleaned up before dinner.

Then if Warren hadn't stopped by for a chat and a beer, it would be dinnertime, once again on the porch. Well, my dinner was on the kitchen floor while TOM was fixing his. Then, when I had finished and his was ready, we would move to the porch so that I could help him eat his dinner.

After a leisurely cup of tea, we'd take another hike while the sun slowly set over the valley in which the lakes rested, returning to the cottage just as dusk would be in full descent.

At this point, we'd pile back into the car for another run into town, perhaps for another coffee on the dock, watching the lake steamer and its crowds return from the day's excursion. Or go window shopping. Or just stroll around watching out for any new tourists. But most often, we'd have to make a run to the market for fresh supplies, since the fridge at the cottage was not overly large.

After returning to the cottage with night having fully fallen, we'd curl up together in a lounge chair, TOM with some book and me next to him with my memories of the day's explorations.

By late evening, it would be time for TOM's stretches and then the newspaper and nightly snack, just like at home in the city. One last leash-free stroll to attend to business and then beddy-bye.

Sounds pretty rigorous, right? Hard to take, eh? Well, I loved it!

Even though our cottages were lake-side, TOM never repeated his Georgia performance in the water, so I never had to watch him make an ass of himself nor feel obligated to go out and rescue him from such odd behavior.

He was vacationing, and therefore so was I. Did I miss the razzle-dazzle of Manhattan, of Second Avenue, of Central Park? Not for a minute. Sure, the pretzels weren't nearly as good. But otherwise, during our too-brief holidays, I enjoyed every minute of them. We only had two of these very special times together, but special indeed they were.

Warren, whom I had known since 1967 when I first moved to Cambridge to begin work at Harvard, had some years later returned to his native home at the southern end of Lake Winnipesaukee, in the charming New England town of Wolfeboro. Those two summers were absolutely delightful. We were blessed both times with splendid weather. The cottages Warren found for us fit our needs perfectly. The scenery was breathtaking. Some of my best and favorite photographs are from those trips. The peace and quiet were eloquent beyond words. It was there that I finally came to understand 'listening to the quiet'. After months of hard work and too-much travel, both summers were completely restorative.

And they have come to mean even more to me since, because the year after our second summer, Warren - my best friend for more than 20 years - unexpectedly died. As much as I still miss him, I'm very lucky to have the memories of those two extended visits.

In ways I do not understand, Warren and Pepper developed a special relationship as well. How else to explain the following?

While he would visit us at our cottage, Pepper and I also spent some evenings with Warren and his wife at their own lake side home a few miles away. As a matter of fact, that's where we had spent our first night after the long drive up from New York, before moving into the cottage the next day.

Now here's the strange part.

At the end of our drive north from Manhattan the second summer, as I turned the car off the highway and into the drive leading down to Warren's home, Pepper - who had spent the whole trip dozing away on the front seat getting his back rubbed, interrupted periodically with 'rest stops' so that each of us could attend to business - jumped up, stood on the seat with his front legs on the window ledge, and raised one excited ruckus.

Now, after a full year's lapse, how the heck did he recognize Warren's driveway?!

Those leisurely summer days lazing away by the lake were as instructive as they were restful. Although I had always pooh-poohed so-called scientists who went off into the wilds to observe animal behavior, I found myself transfixed, observing the pet companion I thought I knew so well in a totally new context.

It was fascinating to watch Pepper get accustomed to his new surroundings. On first arrival and for a few days thereafter, while being completely free to roam and explore at will with no constraining leash, he would only venture so far on his own before turning around to see where I was. Each day while his radius would lengthen from the day before, he would always keep me in a direct line of sight.

As he grew more familiar with his surroundings, as I suppose his confidence grew, he'd not only wander further, but he eventually got to the point where he'd go exploring where he would no longer be able to see me if he turned to look. He had literally as well as figuratively turned a corner. And of course, after a while he was off on his own who knows where.

As for the lake and its contents, while Pepper was no more fond of fresh water than the saltier version, he sure liked being near it. Although he wouldn't go in, he loved to lie on the dock, which extended about ten feet over the water, listening to the gentle waves lap against the pilings and rocky shore line.

Mind you, I liked those docks myself and would park myself there as well. But even if I put myself somewhere else to avoid spend-ing too much time in the sun, he would be down on the dock, stretched out languidly, seemingly at utter peace with the world.

<u>Philly Fido</u>

Late Night News Flash

As I mentioned earlier, at one point TOM was 'between jobs' but – so he claimed - was looking for a new one.

While he may have been out of work, I wasn't. Au contraire, mon ami. That's when he put me to work writing this book - as I've also mentioned if you've been paying attention.

Being so absorbed in keeping him happy by pawing away at the keyboard, I wasn't at all prepared for an announcement TOM made over a year after he had become my full-time human companion.

After nine glorious years in The Big Apple, TOM announced we were moving to Philadelphia.

I learned the news late one night when our newspaper and snacking session was interrupted by a telephone call. It was almost midnight, and you can imagine how startled we both were when the phone rang at that hour.

After hanging up, TOM put his paper down, picked me up, put me in his lap, turned me so we were face to face and announced, "Well Pepper, old man, we're moving to Philadelphia."

Took it calmly, I did. I mean, did I piss in his lap? Crap on his britches? Bite off his nose?

Not cool me. Nope, all I did was stare at the sonofabitch! Struck dumb, I was. Move?!

MOVE!?

Leave New York?!

Leave The Big Apple?!

Leave Central Park?!

For Philadelphia?!

PHILADELPHIA?!

Are you out of your mind?!?!? Is this some kind of joke?!?!?!?

Put me down, you bloody fool.

Hold on here. Just hold on. Let me get this straight.

You're actually serious?

We're supposed to pick up, leave New York, and move to Philadelphia, just like that? No warning? No careful deliber-ation? No weighing of pros and cons? No consultation??!?!?!

Relocation without representation?!

Just what the hell is goin' on here, anyway???????

Damnit, put me down! NOW!!!

As I say, perfectly calm.

Cat crap!

TOM, if you can believe it, actually went back to reading his paper and having his snack. Me? I was no longer interested in even a nibble. My mind was racing, if not the rest of me.

It actually happened just that way. The call from my new boss confirming my position in Philadelphia came at about midnight. And while I had been expecting a call, I wasn't at all certain that the one remaining issue to be resolved would be settled to my satisfaction. I thought the chances no better than 50-50.

When the call did come, it was much later than I had expected and the news was good, quite satisfactory in fact. So the deal was sealed.

The only problem was, well, it was midnight.

Midnight calls are for bad news that can't wait. Good news can always wait, and the next morning would be soon enough to share the news with friends and family. So, after telling Pepper, what else was there to do but to continue poring through the Times?

But don't ask me what I read that night.

To his credit and my relief, once we finally got into bed, he put it all into perspective for me. He told me that while we had some major changes ahead of us and that while our lives were going to be altered in significant ways, the key point - the only really important one - was that we were going to be going through it together. We had each other; it was still us against the world. Together we were more than a match for whatever new challenges and adventures we were about to face.

Drifting off to sleep, I was suffused with the warm glow of love; and only at the periphery was I dimly aware of a tiny voice murmuring, "Philadelphia………."

My Trip to Philly

Moving to Philadelphia was a real trip. Being the creatures of habit that we are, all that disruption was terrifying in anticipation and unsettling in reality, putting it mildly. Trust me, moving's bite is far worse that it's bark.

Moving meant leaving New York. Leaving New York meant leaving the apartment which had been my home all my life - setting aside, as befits them both, my Missouri beginnings and that not-brief-enough sojourn in the Manhattan Pet Store. It meant no more Central Park and Manhattan streets and all my street pals encountered on countless walks. It meant leaving what was known for what was unknown. Scary!

So far as the move itself went, I thought TOM handled that exactly right. What he did was, one night he simply packed my suitcase and took me to Bonnie's. Nothing unusual in that, although it had been some time since TOM had traveled for any extended period of time. He had made a number of brief, typically overnight trips while – allegedly – looking at new jobs, so the appearance of my suitcase and a trip to Bonnie's were not themselves unusual and certainly no cause for alarm.

Little did I know that when I left our apartment that night, I was leaving it for the last time. Truthfully, looking back, I'm very glad I didn't know.

You see, TOM had not yet started to pack in any serious way. Sure, I had seen him clearing out closets, sorting through books, tossing out or giving away all kinds of things. But I figured he had simply decided that it was time for a good spring cleaning and pruning. The place surely needed it since he's more of a

A Dog's Tale

pack-rat than I am; and I never throw anything away. Hell, I've never even buried anything. Not that I haven't tried to, but I soon discovered it's painful and unrewarding on New York's streets and sidewalks.

Spring cleaning? Little did I know or suspect. Yes, he had told me we're "moving to that P place" – which even I knew did not mean a tree or fire hydrant - but how was I to know what that really meant?

I spent two weeks or so at Bonnie's. Even when TOM appeared at Bonnie's door one afternoon – interrupting my nap, dang it - I assumed we were heading back home.

After our usual joyous reunion, he collected my things, and we left. This being mid-afternoon, Bonnie was still at work. We went downstairs for a little walk while I attended to business, and then got into a car that was already waiting for us at the curb.

I just thought TOM had told the cab to wait until he returned. But the car wasn't yellow; when we got into this car, we got into the front seat; and there was no meter but there was a very friendly chap who spoke English who seemed to know TOM quite well. All this got my attention, for sure.

Once underway, we didn't pass any familiar landmarks, didn't pass through Central Park – warning alert! -, and kept going much longer than our typical return trip from Bonnie's. I was now on Full Alert.

Most strangely, a couple of times when we stopped, instead of TOM giving the driver some money, the driver gave money to some stranger at his window. Clearly we were no longer in New York City – proof positive indeed.

Did I mention it was a long ride? Well-over 2 hours – I was keeping an eye on TOM's watch, my anxiety increasing with every circuit of the big and little hands despite TOM's constant petting and stroking.

Meantime, while I'm growing more anxious, TOM and the driver were chatting away like old friends having the best of times.

Something's not right here!!!

Our driver, Bill, was a board member at my new place of work with whom I had become friends during the hiring process and who had been extremely helpful to me in finding a place to live in Philly and with other chores associated with the relocation. When I mentioned I'd be going back to New York to pick up Pepper, he insisted on driving me up and us back.

Bill, a true southern gentleman of the old school, exemplified the Philly concept of brotherly love and was the best of friends for too few years.

Moving and Getting Settled

I knew that for me moving was going to be difficult emotionally as well as logistically. It meant breaking up the New York apartment that Bonnie and I had made into our home. By 1989 when Pepper and I moved, more than a quarter of my life had been spent in that apartment. Many major life changes had taken place in and around it, including Pepper's arrival in my life.

Moving also meant leaving New York City. This was more than just a change in jobs. New city, new home, new friends too. Lots of new chapters to look forward to, but also the closing of just as many.

As disorienting as I expected it to be for me, I thought the same would be true for Pepper, in whatever way a dog experiences such things. I wanted to make it as least disruptive as possible. With that in mind, I thought it best to spare him the experience of watching his home being disrupted; and frankly, it would be a lot easier for me and the movers if he weren't underfoot. So before the real havoc took place, I packed his travel bag and, butt-nips included, delivered him to Bonnie's.

I figured the same would be true at the Philadelphia end as well: best for him not to be around an empty apartment and then underfoot when the movers arrived with our stuff. Bonnie agreed to keep Pepper while I got the new apartment more or less settled.

"More or less" meant that the furniture was essentially placed and most of the cardboard had been cleared away or moved to the sides of the rooms so that you could actually walk from room to room without zig-zagging around boxes.

It was at that mid-way point in the settling in that I figured it was time to fetch the beast. Besides, I was lonely as hell without him!

You'll shortly read Pepper's description of his process of learning about his new home. But watching him explore and discover the layout of the rooms and the paths between them was quite interesting. You could actually watch the learning taking place. Initial uncertainty followed by confusion. Trial and error. Then knowledge. Finally, confidence. May not be as significant or as interesting as watching apes in their natural habitat but it fascinated me.

Our lives together in New York had become so familiar that it had been a long time since I had actually observed Pepper learn something new. Old dogs, new tricks? You bet. And not just Pepper.

First it was the apartment. Then the streets. New routes for his morning and evening walks. For weekend romps. Finding where to go for food, for clean clothes, for drugs, for fresh fruit, for doctors for both of us. For the first months, there were endless discoveries for both of us. Things we were both learning for the first time. Watching Pepper cope and master his new environment gave me courage to continue to do the same with mine.

What I discovered was that the process was the same for both of us. At first everything would take conscious effort. Nothing worked the same way. Nothing could be done on auto pilot. Even muscle memory failed. Turning the same way in the kitchen to open the fridge didn't open the fridge. Getting up in the middle of the night to go to the bathroom didn't get him or me where we needed to be. None of the old habits, routines, rituals, patterns, activities worked quite the same anymore. Everything had to be thought about, tried and mastered. For both of us.

It reminded me of an international student from Latin America in the U.S. for the first time, describing what being in a totally new environment was like. "It's like looking at the world through big eyes," she said. Boy, was she right!

It was all exciting, stimulating, fun, certainly frustrating at times, and tiring. After all, in addition to our shared home life, I was going through the same process at work

I don't ever recall being so exhausted at the end of the day. Every day. There were nights when I simply couldn't stand one more challenge, discovery or new stimulus.

However, for those first several months Pepper was unusually keyed up, almost hyper, with all of the discoveries. It took a good while, months, before he settled back into his normal state of simply being alert and frisky.

We moved in August of 1989. By Christmas time 1990, I was convinced that the upsets, hassles and uncertainties of moving, adjusting and settling in, and for me starting a new job, were behind us and that we were well-positioned to relax and enjoy our new life together.

My New Dog House

As I had feared, when the car finally stopped and we got out, nothing, I mean nothing was familiar. It looked different. It felt different. It smelled different. It was definitely DIFFERENT.

OK, I said to myself. We'll soon be getting back to our apartment. Just pull yourself together; all will be well soon.

Wanna bet?

After a short walk around totally strange surroundings, I was taken into a building I had never seen before, bypassed the elevator right there in the lobby, taken for a walk along a long corridor to the rear of the building where we boarded an elevator, endured a longer ride than usual, and then shown into a completely strange apartment. Did I say "DIFFERENT"?!

Off came my leash and there we were, TOM and me, standing in what looked like a kitchen, looking at each other with quizzical expressions.

Tom at this point looked down and said to me, "Well, what do you think?" While I'm not certain what my expression looked like to him, on the inside I was thinking, "What the hell am I supposed to think?! Where the hell am I and why am I here??!?!?"

So we both just stood there, looking at each other, waiting for the other to move. No way was I about to wander off, since I had no idea of where the hell I was and what surprises or dangers lurked beyond what was obviously kitchen gear, not ours but kitchen gear nonetheless.

He finally moved first, stepping around me to the sink, poured some water into what was at least my water bowl and offered me a drink.

Well, at least it looked like my bowl. But that stuff inside!? Sweet Jesus, it stank! I mean, that stuff wasn't even fit for a dog. I've tasted waters all over the place, some certainly better than others. But nothing, none that reeked anything like what was put before me.

You need to understand that New York's tap water is rightfully acknowledged to be among the world's best tasting and is totally odor-free. It regularly wins contests even against bottled varieties. It's simply The Best.

But that putrid Philly water? YUCK!

Eventually, curiosity – not to mention thirst after the long dry ride - got the best of me: I wanted to see how it would taste given its world class stink. Surprise! It tasted even worse than it smelled. But I digress.......as distinct from digest, especially in this case.

Giving up, TOM picked up the bowl, emptied it in the sink, walked out of the kitchen and urged me to follow.

Follow? Did he think there was one chance in a million - after the day I was having - that I'd do anything but? Stay behind in a strange kitchen with a bowl of some foul-smelling brew that might jump out and assault more than my nostrils at any moment? Follow? He was going to have a hard time keeping me away from his heels which I wanted to be close to for several reasons, not least to be within range of a firm bite – not nip but a full-flesh deep chomp - if he had any more little surprises in store.

Little surprises? Try big ones. Huge ones. Enormous in fact. For what he began to show me was what I was beginning to understand was our new home. I got this idea as we were walking from room to room, because even though the layout was totally new, there was all of the furniture from our New York apartment.

The arm chairs. The sofa. The lounger. Our bed. My toy basket with the collection of my favorite chew sticks, old socks, gloves, rubber doggie toys - mostly for TOM's enjoyment. Everything that I knew so well and that for me meant 'home'.

It was very disorienting, actually. While all the stuff was well-known, it was arranged differently, some even in different rooms. It was as if TOM had spread out our stuff and reshuffled all the pieces which were then redistributed into different rooms.

What's more, there were stacks and stacks of boxes in each room. Large ones. Small ones. Long ones. Short ones. All resting against one or another wall in every room.

Great, I'm thinking, a furnished warehouse! Just what every city-lovin' dog craves. So, I would be spending my future days, TOM out doing whatever it is he does, while I'm on duty as the warehouse watchdog, guarding a bunch of cardboard boxes. Who could ask for anything more?!?!

And doors! I'd never seen so many. Sure, in our New York apartment, every room had a door. You went in and out by the same one. When you left a room, you were back where you had started from.

But not here. In this place most every room had two doors. Even one of the bathrooms! You could walk into a room through one door and leave through another. If you did that, you didn't end up where you had started. You were some place you hadn't been. You tell me that's not disorienting.

And the place was huge, certainly much larger than our apartment in New York. Not only were there more rooms; each one was larger than its counterpart we'd left behind.

For example, the Manhattan kitchen was so small, there was barely enough room for our six feet. Maneuvering around in that kitchen always required complex choreography, where one false step could easily mean a yelp of something other than culinary delight.

Not so the new one. Relative to New York's, it looked like a bowling alley: not terribly wide, but long. Long enough, in fact, for me to do my "touch and go's" well-away from the risk of contaminating more conventional kitchen activities.

"Touch and go's"?

TOM at one point had learned to fly an airplane, and to do that, he explained that you had to practice takeoffs and landings a lot, known as 'touch and go's'. Well, the yoke's on him: my 'touch and go's' are when I use newspapers for certain bodily functions.

In New York, the rear hall where the back door was – well away from the kitchen - had been pressed into service. But in Philly, the back door – closest to the elevators – entered into the kitchen, and it was long enough to afford ample space for my touch and goes to be near the door but far enough away from the kitchen appliances not to pose a problem, real or imagined.

All of the other rooms had been on steroids as well. Take the living room, for example. In Manhattan's, it was possible, indeed practical to get from an arm chair to the sofa, or vice versa without intermediate use of the floor, and from there to our lounger with two steps on the floor. Think 'compact'.

Try that in the new place and you know what would happen? A belly flop in the middle of the carpet. Or a crushed nose against a table that isn't where it had been, or is supposed to be. Think 'spacious'.

Or I could jump off the bed in New York and be at the front door pronto. In Philadelphia, it seems like half my walk is over before I even make it to the door. This may not seem like such a big deal to you. But in my case, it means that in addition to retooling my muscle memory, my bladder needed to be retrained as well.

Even the layout, the relationship of one room to another, is different. The scheme in New York had been that all rooms opened off of a central hall: kitchen to the left; bedroom to the right; den straight ahead. Not so now. No such luck. Here things are what you call L-shaped but what we call dog-legged.

Back in New York, there was only one way in and out of each room. But in Philly, in addition to the L-shape so that all rooms faced the outside there is also an interior hallway and two-doors-per-room. That means that there are two alternative routes to get from one place to another.

Talk about confusing! Although I have to admit that once I mastered it, it has made for some really terrific games of Hide and Seek. TOM and I have always had fun playing this game. I'm always 'it' while TOM gets to hide. In New York, I could always rely on the fact that once I had confirmed Tom was not lurking within a room, I could eliminate it as a hiding place.

Not so now, damnit. With alternative means of escaping each room, it's possible for TOM to change his hiding place while I'm still searching.

Of course whenever I really want to, I can easily find him following his scent. But he seems to enjoy the illusion of escaping immediate detection, so I play along. The new apartment has made this little deception more pawsible, er, plausible. It's fun for me to let TOM think he's winning. But only up to a point. Have to careful with him.

Another thing about my new home: the flooring. As I said, TOM brought along all the old furniture. I soon discovered that he also brought along all the area rugs. Great. More familiar things. But just one little problem.

If you have the same amount of carpeting but a lot more space, know what you've got? Right! A lot of slippery wood floors all newly-polyurethaned so that the surface is as treacherous as an ice rink. And you know what that means? Slips. Slides. Impossible stops and turns. Banged up nose, hips, jaw and damned near every other body part. Worst of all: acute embarrassment and bruised ego!

As that preacher-man would have said, "If God had wanted you to skate, he'd a put skates on your paws!"

Frankly I should admit that I'm glad to have made this move when I am a bit older, wiser and – yes, let's be honest, slower – than in my rampaging puppy years. No question I'm a bit better equipped to deal with – and more respectful of – the ice rink flooring that is now mine to tread upon than I would have been earlier on. Imagine: Thar' he goes!!

Along with its other charms, there is one overwhelmingly positive feature to the new apartment: two sets of large French doors, one each in the living and dining/office rooms, opening onto a sunny southern exposure. Translation? Plenty of fresh air and sunlight.

The New York apartment had many wonderful features, but fresh air and sunlight sadly were not among them. It was not an accident that some of our friends referred to that place as The Dungeon.

But they would never be able to say that about our new place. Quite the contrary.

And TOM has thoughtfully placed two little carpets in front of each set of doors with me in mind. You'd better believe they quickly have become my favorite spots. I can lie for hours, basking in the sun, caressed by gentle breezes. Even on the coldest of winter days, as long as the sun is shining and the light is pouring through those doors, I can stretch out on the carpet and feel the warming rays of the sun.

Maybe moving to Philadelphia may not be so bad after all.

Park vs Park

One of my worst fears about leaving The Big Apple was no longer being able to enjoy Central Park – what I had come to regard as our back yard - what fun and adventures we had there.

Well, guess what? In lieu of Central Park, we now have Fairmount Park, which, it turns out, is the largest urban park in the country. I mean, it goes for miles and miles and miles. It actually starts right in the central part of the city, only several blocks from where we live and then winds its way through various parts of the city and out into the suburbs.

Because it is so large and since the population here is less than in New York, Fairmount Park is not nearly as overused, or abused, as Central Park. People here seem to treat their environment and particularly their Park with more respect, not debasing it with their graffiti and garbage nearly as much.

On our long walks in our new Park on the many hiking trails we haven't once passed anyone carrying a boom-box blasting "music" to wreck the pastoral setting and pleasure. Nor, I hasten to add, is the Park patrolled by Mounted Gestapo. If there is a leash law, no one – including us – pays the least attention.

On the other hand, I do miss the illicit delight of thumbing my snout – and butt – at the Authorities.

Every weekend TOM and I head off to Fairmount Park for our hikes. Although these excursions are in one sense less interesting that our strolls in Central Park - fewer encounters with sticky-fingered babies, for example - they are more enjoyable. Literally, walks in the countryside. Very much like being in New Hampshire's woods. But now, every weekend. Delightful!

To add icing on this cake, not too long after settling in, TOM got us our own car! Imagine: no more waiting impatiently for a cab. And also imagine having the freedom to explore many more parts of the Park. Besides, I get to sit up front with a better view. And, someone needs to make sure TOM is going in the right direction.

On the other paw, with a clear view of city traffic, there are many times when I happily curl up on the seat, or better yet in the foot well, and doze versus gripping the dashboard or window ledge in sheer terror.

What I mean by that is the drivers in the Big Apple were crazy but crazy with a plan. Here in Philly, they're just plain crazy. Let me put it this way, whatever brotherly love exists in Philly ends at the curb.

More about the car later, but yes, having our own transportation enabled us to enjoy many parts of Fairmount Park. One became a particular favorite, called 'Forbidden Drive'; and we returned there often.

It is a trail which follows the Wissahickon Creek which runs the length of the Park. Unlike the trail heads originating in the City which tend to be rather crowded, the section of Forbidden Drive which we enjoy is accessed about mid-Park and while popular is not the least bit crowded. Quite the contrary. We'd pack a lunch, set off for the Park in the morning, and spend most of the day wandering along the Drive and following its many trails. More so than Central Park, being on the Drive was every-bit like being in New Hampshire's bucolic woods. It's a toss-up who enjoys these outings more, Pepper or me.

I'll not comment on Pepper's navigational skills, but his observations about Philly's drivers are, sadly, quite accurate.

The Square vs The Streets

In addition to our new home, there were of course many more adjustments to be made.

For example, I had expected to sorely miss the familiar scents of Second Avenue relished every night after dinner. But to my delight, Philly offered something better.

Living where we do, we have only a two-block walk to Rittenhouse Square, one of four magnificent central city mini-parks with which this town is blessed.

The Square is a bucolic landscape full of majestic old trees, interior walkways, lovingly maintained gardens, a fountain, benches, and lots and lots of people and other dogs. And while the posted regulations require that we be kept on leashes, TOM - as soon as we cross over into the Square – sets me free.

Every night after dinner TOM and I head for this oasis. Nightly instead of only on weekends, I am off the leash and free to roam, romp, sniff, mark, explore, frolic to my heart's content. Every night. Seven days a week. Every week. Heaven!

Sure, once in a while an officer of the law stops and instructs TOM to put me back on the leash. But as soon as he is out of sight, I'm set free again.

Let me give you an example of how Philly differs from New York. I described earlier our encounters with the authorities in Central Park. Mounted, they bring to mind a Galloping Gestapo: rude, pushy, unquestionably authoritarian even by New York standards.

But when stopped in the Square here in Philly, the person in uniform says with the greatest politeness, "Excuse me, Sir, but would you please put your dog on his leash? Thank you very much. Have a pleasant evening."

It almost makes me feel guilty when I re-release Pepper shortly thereafter.

While surrounded by one-way vehicular traffic, there are no particularly noisy cars or trucks. Therefore no cloud of exhaust fumes assaulting my sensitive snout. No hoard of commuters hell-bent on trampling anything and everything in their paths, even critters like me.

It's green, not grey; and while I am understandably partial to grey, even I admit you can get too much of a good thing.

There certainly are just as many dogs here with whom to play and whose scents can be explored and enjoyed. People-watching is even more fun, since the ones here are leisurely strolling along in various attire, rather than forced-marching in full business dress.

There are loads of benches along the many criss-crossing paths on which to sit and people and pet watch and/or drink in the views of either the lighted towers of the business district or the lighted homes of the apartments, including ours, or of the luxury hotel or even of the 19th century townhouses where TOM works.

In short, every night is a treat.

Until of course winter sets in. Then all bets are off and most differences disappear. Snow, ice, slush and – damnit – salt are just as prevalent here as back there. Take my whimper for it: Philly's salt is just as painful and bountiful as New York's. Brotherly love indeed?!?!?!

The sad but universal truth is that salt stings.

Philly Blemishes

Philly's salt is not its only phault, 'er fault. For example, back in New York TOM took me along on his nightly errands including grocery shopping. Not so here. Sure, he tried it at first. Tucked me under his arm and in we went as we had in New York. Didn't get five paces. "Out!", the manager insisted, politely but firmly.

Okay, so we tried another market. "Out!", again. Cripes! How inhospitable. Henceforth I've been left at home when TOM goes for the goodies.

Or street noises. If you live in New York City, every day is a balancing act, trying to find enough good to offset the inherently bad. Like noise. Even though our apartment in New York was on the back of the building and mid-block, we were still bombarded with street noises. And of all the ones that ground away on our nerves, the garbage trucks at 5 a.m. were the worst. I can't tell you how much I looked forward, once settled in Philadelphia, to not having those daily audible assaults.

Surprise! Even though our new apartment is on a higher floor, we are right over a main street. And you remember those beautiful French doors I told you about? Guess what they let in, in addition to fresh air and sunshine? Yup, the grinding and crashing of garbage trucks in the wee hours. Double Damn!!

Speaking of higher floors and elevators, our new apartment building is larger, much larger. Higher and larger carries three important consequences for me. One is more crowded elevator rides meaning my tender feet are at greater risk. They also mean slower rides, much slower rides, each one a local it seems. And last but definitely not least, it is further, much further to the front door. And I am not getting any younger. What used to be merely pressing business is now of greater, much greater urgency.

My mornings which used to be casually pleasant are now almost always cross-eyedly anxious. Not a great way to start the day.

And once outside, there are far fewer fellow canines among the locals than back in good ol' New York. There I had lots of street buddies; here, not so much. What was common there is rare here, which I find both lonely and rather disconcerting.

And to be honest, the local bipeds aren't nearly as friendly as their cousins to the north. It's not that they are reserved or distant so much as just downright snooty. Like I'm not good enough to be walking on their sidewalk. Like their crap smells better'n mine!

The good side about that Chilly Philly crowd is that the few really open and warm hearted ones, both canines and bipeds are extremely welcoming and delightful to be with. It's true, a few really good friends are better than many casual acquaintances.

But those few glitches aside, I have found the move to Philadelphia very much to my liking. In almost all respects, my new life is better than the delightful one I left behind in New York.

No one is more surprised by this than me. You know how much I loved my life in New York. Sure, up to that point it had been the only one I had known, so I had nothing to compare it to. Even so, my life with TOM in New York had been wonderful.

Naturally I worried about that when it came time to build a new life in Philadelphia. And now all I can say is that, wonder of wonders, it's even better here! With all the changes and adjustments made and with a new, even more wonderful life together with TOM, I am looking forward to the future with complete contentment.

I'm one lucky dog!

<u>Diagnosis and Care</u>

The Bombshell

By the winter of 1990, Philadelphia had become 'home'. I was increasingly comfortable and at ease at work and at home. As far as I could tell, Pepper seemed to have adjusted happily to his new life as well. All the hassles of the move and settling in for both of us were behind us. A promising future beckoned.

Unbelievably, it was that very spring that brought the most devastating of all possible news: Pepper was diagnosed with a terminal illness.

Beginning in late April, his behavior had started to change in strange ways. First he began to consume a great deal of water. This in turn meant that he began to use his papers much more frequently.

Then his sleeping pattern changed dramatically. Rather than spending the night cuddled in my arms sleeping soundly, he began to toss and turn all night. Like he couldn't find a comfortable position.

But the most alarming sign was when he began to jump off the bed and walk the perimeter of the apartment and then jump back on the bed. Not a casual stroll from room to room, but a deliberate tracing of the edges of each room. He'd toss and turn for about an hour and then go for another perimeter walk.

Greatly concerned after two nights of this, I took him to his customary vet. Pepper's heart rate was found to be abnormally low, as was his blood sugar.

Thinking the heart the more serious of the two, the vet prescribed medication to quicken the heartbeat, taught me how to take Pepper's pulse, and sent us home.

The heart medication had very little measurable benefit on Pepper's pulse rate, and it did nothing to improve his pattern of sleep and perimeter walking.

Now more distressed, I took Pepper to be examined at the Small Animal Hospital of the University of Pennsylvania, the teaching and research hospital associated with the top-rated University's

School of Veterinary Medicine.

After I described his symptoms and provided the doctor with his recent medical history, I was asked to leave Pepper overnight for further detailed examination and observation.

It was the next night, the 8th of May 1990 that the doctor called with the news. Pepper's liver was shrinking. I was told that unlike enlarging livers which can be successfully treated and the damage reversed, a shrinking liver cannot be 'cured'. It is an untreatable and terminal condition; only the symptoms can be managed. They also referred me to a specialist whose practice dealt solely with such issues.

As scattered and random and unpredictable my thoughts, my feelings were even more so. So many different feelings. So strong. From different angles. Fear. Fright. Anger. Sadness. Bitterness. Overwhelming love and compassion for Pepper. Enormous black holes of nothingness, voids deep in my gut. Worries about him. About me. About us. On and on and on.

I thought it might help if I kept some sort of journal; I even began one. Here's how I started.

The Journal

17 May 1990

As I write this, my dog is dying. Just eight days ago I was given the devastating news. My 11-year-old miniature Schnauzer Pepper has been diagnosed as having a terminal liver problem. While the details may be of some interest and will be duly reported subsequently, the inescapable bottom line is that the end of his life is imminent.

There is no way of accurately predicting how quickly the liver will deteriorate, nor of estimating what additional complications will develop, and therefore no firm estimate of the amount of time we have left together. The 'best case' scenario is months, perhaps a year at the outside, and the 'worst case' is a matter of weeks.

At the moment he does not yet have any serious complicating factors for which he tests positive or negative. So there is some reason to hope that we may be blessed with a longer rather than shorter time frame. But medicine is still very much an art and not a science; there can be no certain, firm predictions.

The pronouncement of this death sentence has altered my life in ways I have yet to know. Surely in the last week I have thought about, worried over little else. The news, the changes in Pepper's behavior, the alterations in his diet and care have pre-occupied every waking moment, and very likely many unconscious ones as well.

As I try to adjust to these new realities and try to fend off all of the dreaded and dreadful imaginings about what is to come, I have decided to keep this diary of our last journey together. We have shared so much these past 11 years, our lives have been so intimately intertwined, this little loving creature has been so much my emotional anchor that I honestly don't know how I will be able to cope with what lies ahead.

I mean, I know I will somehow find the strength to try to give him the best possible care and to sustain the best possible quality of life for him as long as is reasonably possible. Caring for him and ministering to his needs, making whatever adjustments will be required in my life and routine will be the easier, not easy but more manageable part.

What I am less confident about, and why a diary seems like a good idea, is the emotional part. In ways that perhaps only other devoted animal lovers can understand, the psychological and emotional blows and adjustments and highs and lows can only be imagined, which is to say, feared.

Accepting his imminent loss, worrying about potential pain and discomfort and deterioration in the quality of his life, facing the probable decision of when to apply euthanasia, going through with that act and then trying to deal with my life without him, at least from this entry point it all seems overwhelming.

Perhaps this meager effort to describe, to record, to explain, and to understand and then ultimately accept will help me cope along the way. I surely hope so.

In the last analysis, I cannot alter the inevitable, painful, damnable reality. Pepper is dying and will die soon. No matter how much, how fervently I pray that this is not so, there is no escaping the awful truth.

For most of my life I have been successful at finding my way around, over or through all types of problems and hurdles. Basically I have come to believe that, given enough creativity and hard work, there isn't anything, any problem that cannot be solved, beaten, bested. I really got to thinking that Vince Lombardi, long-time and very successful head coach of the Green Bay Packers was right: You never lost a football game; you simply ran out of time. Until now I figured that there was even a way to beat the clock.

But death is, as they say, final. For the first time in my 47 years, I'm face-to-face with a situation that cannot be beaten, a problem that cannot be solved, a hurdle that cannot be surmounted.

Now there is no chance. The best veterinarians working with the most modern equipment and up-to-date medical knowledge hold out no hope. Pepper's condition is untreatable, irreversible and terminal. And so for the first time in my life, I come face to face with the harshest, most painful truth of all: I am totally and completely helpless – Nature will take its own course.

What's even worse is that the one thing I have held, do hold, the most dear is where I must learn this Life lesson. There is nothing, nothing I can do to alter the reality of Pepper's impending death. To do nothing while watching the most important thing in my life die in front of my very eyes and possibly, with luck, in my own arms……the ache is soul deep.

And there is yet another aching lesson to be learned: To live without hope. Never before have I had to live without hope. No matter how difficult, complex, complicated, and even apparently futile life's twists and turns have been or seemed, I have chosen to believe that there is always hope.

Hope is what keeps us going in the face of odds, great and small.

Regardless of how grim present circumstances appear, our feet hit the floor in the morning because - one way or another somehow - we believe that there is the possibility of a better day; that there is, after all, reason to hope.

And while I know that my own life will continue, for Pepper there can be no such hope. That he may not yet and may never grasp that reality gives me some small comfort.

The vets tell me I can manage his symptoms and presumably thereby manage the level of discomfort he may come to experience. With luck, he will never sense the hopelessness of his condition.

This is a burden I alone have to shoulder. I don't honestly know if I can. Hopefully this journal of our final journey together will help. I undertake it as an effort to come to grips with my pain and grief, and perhaps thereby learn to live these next weeks, perhaps months, helpless and without hope.

I love him so, and it hurts so much.

*   *   *   *   *

27 June 1990

So what's the problem? Simple, really. Deceptively, fatally simple. Pepper's liver is shrinking. The doctors don't know the cause. Indeed, they say that whatever the reason for the reduction, it wouldn't make any difference in either his treatment or his prognosis. Regardless of what has caused, may still be causing, his liver to shrink, this physical fact and whatever as yet unknown complications it may trigger will cause his death.

There are, the specialist says, many possible causes for a shrinking liver. Unlike tumors, benign or otherwise, and other factors that can cause a liver to increase in size, in the case of a reducing liver, nothing can be done to reverse the deterioration nor to forestall its progress. He says that in this case all that can be done is to manage the symptoms. And all the vets have said that the best case is months, perhaps as much as a year, and the worst case is weeks.

The good news is that, so far, Pepper hasn't yet tested positive or

*negative for any of the signs that would lead the specialist to ex-
pect the worst case scenario.*

*Adding to the mystery is the unknown of how long the disease
has been underway. The vets say that a shrinking liver has many
possible causes and may actually have been underway for a sub-
stantial period of time. It is possible that the rest of Pepper's
body could have been compensating for his shrinking liver for
some time.*

*Naturally I have asked whether there would have been warning
signs or symptoms that I should have detected sooner. All the
doctors have been reassuring on this point, since in all likelihood the compensating that may have been taking place effec-
tively masked any problems and would have prevented an earlier
diagnosis.*

*So they say. But of course I can't help but wonder. Wonder and
worry. What if I had picked up the signs sooner? Wouldn't that
have enabled them, the vets and medical science, to work their
wonders earlier and therefore with greater effect on Pepper's
longevity?*

*Cause and effect. There is the essential human need to under-
stand both, and the relationship between them. What started the
problem; what was the initial cause of Pepper's shrinking liver?*

*That is apparently never to be known. I don't know how I will be
able to live with that ignorance, how I cannot, will not fill that
void with the worse possible imaginings.*

*The ultimate effect, however, is known: Pepper's death. This is
knowledge of certitude. That it is definitive is of absolutely no
comfort whatsoever. Indeed the certain anticipation of the inevitable is painful to the core of my being.*

*So long as death was but an abstraction, some event that while
inevitable one could always imagine as far off and therefore
somehow beatable, it permitted denial and allowed - false to be
sure - hope. If not ultimate hope, still some expectation that the
end was a distant, far removed reality permitting life's full
measure of joy in the interim.*

But a death sentence, even one so vaguely worded as "weeks, months, perhaps a year", removes any rational basis for denial, eliminates any false hopes, erases an open-ended future.

Even on his good days, when Pepper may still show his customary pep and vigor and playfulness, even then I will know the fearful reality.

It won't be easy.

Pepper's Care

While I seemed unwilling if not unable to come to grips emotionally with the hard realities of Pepper's terminal illness, I became absorbed in trying to understand the medical facts. Perhaps if I could intellectually grasp the reasons for Pepper's pending death, that knowledge would help me cope with the emotional enormity of his loss.

I came to understand that the liver's decreasing effectiveness meant that Pepper's body was changing in many ways, the most important being changes in his blood chemistry. Among those, the most serious was the inability to process protein properly, so that damaging levels of certain chemicals would increasingly alter or inhibit the functioning of his brain. Not brain damage in a physical sense, but chemical harm, producing changes in behavior and, more important, proper functioning of other parts of his body.

Although nothing could be done to stop or cure the disease, managing the consequences proved deceptively simple. All that was necessary was to reduce the amount of protein entering Pepper's body, and to speed up the digestive process with a laxative to permit less time for harmful chemical processes to be initiated.

Since his liver continued to shrink, the balance between what protein he could safely be given and the amount of laxative to accompany it would require continuous monitoring and adjusting. Once a 'safe' level was established, he would be okay, meaning no extreme symptoms such as seizures, restless tossing and turning at night, or perimeter walking.

There would be no way of estimating how long Pepper would remain at any given level of protein/laxative. He might be fine for a month or so, or perhaps only a few weeks. Then once the symptoms recurred, it would necessitate a further reduction in protein and an increase in the laxative, until a new safe level was established. And then the cycle would repeat itself.

At one of the early stages when an adjustment was needed, the doctors suggested that I break his daily intake into two smaller meals, rather than the one large which had been his custom. So, for the first time since he had been a puppy, Pepper got both breakfast and dinner. However this little deception didn't last long before a further protein reduction was needed.

For a while, I was able to feed him specially manufactured canned dog food. There are actual preparations just for cases such as his. He had been given one version of this series ever since his pancreatic problem as a puppy, a mixture of chicken and rice. The next stages in the series of these preparations altered the balance by decreasing the chicken and increasing the rice proportions.

Each time it was necessary to reduce further the amount of protein, he would shift down to the next level of the series. And the amount of liquid laxative that would be poured over his food would be increased.

But eventually he was unable to tolerate the preparation with the lowest level of protein. At that point, in the absence of any commercially available options, the doctors suggested a diet of either boiled rice or a cold baked potato. After trying both, Pepper seemed to prefer the potato.

Other than the changes in his diet and the laxative, there was only one medication to be administered. It was a pill taken with each meal and at bedtime to inhibit bleeding, in the event he had an internal hemorrhage. The danger, the doctors explained, was more from the high level of protein in the blood which could cause a terminal brain problem in the event of a hemorrhage than death from loss of blood itself. Thus something to inhibit any bleeding that might take place was a preventive measure, just in case. And I was instructed to monitor his stools with care, to be on the lookout for any traces of internal bleeding.

At one point, Pepper began to show signs of difficulty in chewing. It was at that stage that I discovered that there are veterinary dentists, one of whom at the Penn Small Animal Hospital was asked to examine Pepper. His conclusion was that Pepper had developed an infection in his mouth from a problem with a couple of his front teeth. Under normal circumstances, the teeth would have been extracted. But since Pepper's liver condition precluded extraction as an option - a reduced liver, it turns out, is unable to handle any of the anesthetics used in surgery - an antibiotic was added to his medicinal intake.

And that was all I could do. Given the enormity of what was happening, it was too little and too easy and too simple. I felt I should be doing more, and was enormously frustrated. While the doctors were reassuring that I was doing all that could be done, and even though I almost accepted that judgement intellectually, I never quite accepted it emotionally.

Other than his diet and two pills with each meal, and with the encouragement of Pepper's medical team, I resolved to try to maintain as much of his normal routine as possible, for as long as possible.

We still went for our many walks both in the Square and on Forbidden Drive, even if they weren't as extended as they had been. Although he may have moved less quickly, he was no less eager to go and just as interested in exploring as always.

He actually put on a little weight and retained his fluffy coat. Seeing him on the street, you never would have known he was terminally ill. At most you might have thought that he was showing his age a bit, which at 13 wouldn't have been all that surprising under the best of circumstances.

As his strength waned and he was no longer able to do it himself, I would lift him onto and down from the bed or lounge chair. Since I couldn't be around all day every day, I would leave a seat cushion from the sofa and his blanket on the floor, so he would still have his little nook during the day.

Treats became pieces of toast, which he consumed as eagerly as commercial dog biscuits or samples of my own meals. And since he no longer could have any of my other food, I made certain I had some toast with every meal, pieces of which were substituted for his snippets of my food...and he never seemed to notice or mind the difference. If I didn't move my hand quickly enough, the tips of my fingers remained in danger.

And he still had to endure his nightly abuse with the brush.

Worse, at some point I no longer felt comfortable taking him to the groomers, as I feared that the added stress of that experience would not be good for him. Since his coat continued to grow, there came a time when there was no alternative but for me to play barber. You can imagine, given how Pepper felt about being brushed, what he must have endured once I started on him with a pair of scissors.

I had resolved from the very beginning that I would do anything and everything I could to maintain the quality of Pepper's life for as long as possible. I might not know how long that would be. I had to accept the possibility that the end could come at any time. But what I did know was that I was going to do whatever I could to assure that his last days, however many there were going to be, would be as enjoyable as possible for him.

And even though I knew there was the possibility that Nature might intervene, there was a stronger likelihood that at some point I would have to make a decision that I knew how to think about but had no idea at all how to cope with emotionally.

Loving him as I did, I knew that the basis for deciding about euthanasia, while painful in the extreme, was really quite simple. I could not, I would not, let him suffer.

When it was clear that the quality of his life had diminished or that his discomfort had increased, then it would be time.

I knew that in my head. My heart couldn't bear it.

At one point, I asked the doctors how to judge when it would be time. And what about hope? What about the possibility that he might get better, bounce back, rally, if only for a short time? How do you know when it really is time?

Certainly part of me was wanting the vets to assume the responsibility. If only they could give me a formula I could follow, then the full weight of the awful decision would not be mine.

Pepper's doctors were simply wonderful and had been throughout. No one could have asked for more sensitive, caring, supportive, responsive, and thoughtful medical professionals. They had been as willing to treat me as they had been to care for Pepper. But on this crucial question, they could not give me what I wanted. All they could say was that I would know when it was time. Pepper would tell me, they said.

And eventually he did.

The Passing

Saying Goodbye

Pepper seemed in good spirits and presumably was not in any pain, measured by the vigor with which he consumed his meals, until the evening of February 12, 1992. However, his decline was quite rapid that night and throughout the next day.

In May of 1990 when his liver condition was detected and judged terminal, the doctors thought the best case would be months, perhaps be a year.

Thankfully, he lived for almost two; and until the 12th the quality of his life and sweetness of character were not adversely affected by his steadily diminishing strength, stamina and senses. The neurological damage seemed to affect only his behavior, not his personality. Until the last night, he was alert, interested in his world and as full of love and loving as always.

In addition to all the years we had shared, with the major life changes that took place after Pepper came into my life, he became an even more treasured companion. How treasured?

Let me share a story.

Early in our life together and during one of our evening walks, we met up with one of our street friends. While I of course never had exchanged names with this guy and have forgotten the name of his pet companion, something that gentleman said to me that night has stayed with me.

While the two dogs were doing their sniffing and circling thing, he and I got to talking about how we came to have our pet companions and discovered similar circumstances. He went on to say that he had subsequently gotten divorced and that, referring to his pet companion, "He saved my life."

Our dogs soon decided it was time to move on, each in their own directions. I remember thinking at the time what an odd thing I'd just heard. This guy who was an imposing physical presence at comfortably over six feet with a bass voice that seemed to spring up from his feet, looked and sounded totally in command of his life. Yet his dog had saved his life? It just didn't make sense to me.

When Bonnie and I went our separate ways not too long after this chance meeting, as I began experiencing and trying to adjust to my new life, I began to get a glimmer of understanding of what that street friend had said. Pepper's place in my life became greatly enlarged, so much so that I began to not just understand what had been said, I began to think and feel the same way. And as each year went by, that truth came larger and stronger, even as the pain of the split-up slowly receded.

Moreover, Pepper was not only a source of emotional support but also a needed distraction. No matter how self-absorbed or obsessed I might be about my own problems, Pepper had to be cared for. Walked. Fed. Yes, even brushed. My responsibilities to and for him kept me from being completely focused on my own needs and hurt.

The complete and unqualified love we enjoy from our pet companions is always a dear and precious thing, but much more so in times of emotional distress and vulnerability.

At least in my case that heightened bond formed in crisis remained and grew stronger as the crisis dimmed and eventually disappeared.

And beyond those crises, we had shared and enjoyed so many wonderful times and adventures together, up and down the East Coast, hoodwinking New York City's Finest, disrupting Yuppies brunches, dozing by New Hampshire lakes, chasing wild rabbits in Georgia, watching all the crazy animals - only some on four legs - in Central Park, working the streets of The Big Apple, quiet evenings in our lounge chair, falling asleep curled up together.....we had had a wonderful, rich and fulfilling life together for almost 13 years.

What's more, at the time of Pepper's final illness, our relationship had become the longest sustained one of my life. Little wonder, then, that I had come to fully understand and appreciate the breadth and depth of the role of my one true Best Friend.

'Grateful' doesn't begin to describe how I felt about my years with Pepper. He had given me so much and been so much a part of my life.

And it was because of all that he had given me for so long that I was able to summon the will and strength and love to arrange for him to be euthanized as soon as it was clear his quality of life had markedly dimmed even though all my other instincts were to hang on to him as long as possible.

After giving the go-ahead nod to the vet to insert the needle and cradling Pepper wrapped in a blanket in my arms, I could feel his quick passage as I murmured into his ear one last, "I love you, Pepper."

A Dog's Tale

About the Author

Ron Wormser enjoyed a fascinating 40-year career in executive positions in higher education, international student exchanges, administrative support for international applied agricultural research centers and a classical music training and performing arts institution. With his wife, Marian, he retired and relocated from the East Coast to the Monterey Peninsula where he maintains an active consulting practice with local nonprofits.

In his 70's, he is indulging his long-delayed interest in writing with the publication by BoardSource in 2015 of *Informed Fundraising*, a primer for decision-makers responsible for raising funds for nonprofits. Now with *A Dog's Tale*, a joint undertaking begun some years ago with his beloved miniature Schnauzer, Pepper, his second book makes its debut. It is a story told almost entirely from Pepper's perspective about his life first in New York City and then in Philadelphia, with occasional contributions from Ron.

While human companions may be startled and amused by a canine's perspective on the world shared with their pets, mostly it is a story about Pepper and Ron's relationship, and the special bond between two species. It is a book for every pet-lover and for all those who aren't but who want or need to understand those of us who are.

Other books at SetonPublishing.com

- by Tony Seton

Mokki's Peak

Silent Alarm

Deki-san

Equinox

No Soap, Radio

Paradise Pond

Selected Writings

The Brink

Jennifer

The Francie LeVillard Mysteries - Vol I-IX

Trinidad Head

Dead as a Doorbell

Just Imagine

Musings on Sherlock Holmes

The Autobiography of John Dough, Gigolo

Silver Lining

Mayhem

The Omega Crystal

Truth Be Told

The Quality Interview / Getting it Right
    on Both Sides of the Mic

From Terror to Triumph /
    The Herma Smith Curtis Story

Don't Mess with the Press / How to Write, Produce, and
    Report Quality Television News

Right Car, Right Price

- *by other authors*

A Rich & Valued Life - Martin C. Needler

The Enchanted Emerald - Donald Craghead

The Dedicated Life of an American Soldier - Ray Ramos

Life Is a Bumpy Road - Tony Albano

From Hell to Hail Mary / A Cop's Story - Frank DiPaola

From Colored Town to Pebble Beach /
*   The Story of the Singing Sheriff - Pat DuVal*

The Early Troubles - Gerard Rose

The Boy Captain - Gerard Rose

Bless Me Father - Gerard Rose

For I Have Sinned - Gerard Rose

A Western Hero - Gerard Rose

Red Smith in LA Noir - David Jones

The Shadow Candidate - Rich Robinson

Hustle is Heaven - Duncan Matteson

Vision for a Healthy California - Bill Monning

Three Lives of a Warrior - Phil Butler

Live Better Longer - Hugh Wilson

Green-Lighting Your Future / How You Can
*   Manifest the Perfect Life - John Koeberer*

47452216R00103

Made in the USA
San Bernardino, CA
30 March 2017